Caché

Objects

and

Atelier

Caché Objects and Atelier

There are many good MUMPS developers who want to learn Caché Objects but do not know where to start.

At the same time InterSystems is pushing the envelope of technology with a new development platform such as Atelier along with Eclipse.

It is my aim in this book to help those developers bridge the gap into Caché Objects at the same time learn Atelier as well.

This book is an introduction into Caché Objects and Atelier but not a fully developed instruction manual.

In teaching Objects and Atelier, I compare Classes and Routines between Caché Studio and Atelier.

InterSystems Caché®

InterSystems Caché® is an advanced database management system and rapid application development environment. With Caché, you'll make breakthroughs in processing and analyzing complex Big Data, and developing Web and mobile applications. Caché uniquely offers lightning-fast performance, massive scalability, and robust reliability – with minimal maintenance and hardware requirements.

Caché is a new generation of database technology that provides multiple modes of data access. Data is only described once in a single integrated data dictionary and is instantly available using object access, high-performance SQL, and powerful multidimensional access – all of which can simultaneously access the same data.

Caché comes with several built-in scripting languages and is compatible with the most popular development tools.

 - Based on promotional material from the InterSystems website: *www.InterSystems.com*

Object Technology

Object Technology is a new way to look at data processing. Simply put, an Object is data and the code that changes that data in one unit, or one object.

In legacy applications, data was separated from the code that changed the data.

By combining data and changes, we have a more complete, and manageable representation of the data combined with the modifying code. This is a paradigm shift that traditional data processing has been undergoing for the past several decades and will continue for the foreseeable future.

InterSystems Caché Atelier

Caché Atelier is the next generation of development environment for InterSystems. As a plug-in to Eclipse, Atelier is a step-up from Caché Studio (the earlier development environment). It is my hope that this book will make mastering Object Technology and Atelier a little easier and quicker for developers.

Mike Kadow 2018

Formatting

A word about formatting, I wrote this book to flow nicely regardless of the output device. As such, elongated white spaces may be seen at the bottom of a page. I have done this to keep logical examples together, which should aid in the reader's comprehension.

Screen Shots

It was difficult to display screen shots in a uniform manner and still make them readable. As such, their size may seem sporadic and irregular. For this I apologize.

Dedication

I dedicate this book to my lovely wife of over 41 years.

"Charm is deceitful, and beauty is vain, but a woman who fears the LORD is to be praised." Book of Proverbs 31:30

I am truly blessed!

Special Thanks

Dick Martel, my friend and mentor

Who coined the phrase, "Crashed and burning on the learning curve."

InterSystems Corporation

I am also indebted to InterSystems Corporation for their excellent documentation, examples, and support center. It is this attitude for openness from InterSystems that spreads the Caché message and technology.

Editors: Paul Bradney and Robert Cemper

Both Paul and Robert have provided me with invaluable advice and assistance in the writing of this book and help me to realize to look outside of myself. Thank you for being there.

**Printed and Distributed
by CreateSpace.**

ISBN-13:978-1548002220

ISBN-10:1548002224

Table of Contents

Chapter 1 - Overview

Purpose

The purpose of this book is to help the Caché/MUMPS/M developer quickly become proficient with Caché Objects and/or the Atelier development environment along with Eclipse.

The author has two goals; 1) teach Caché Objects and 2) teach the Atelier development environment along with Eclipse. These two goals are taught together and as such the book may seem mixed up at times.

Since Atelier is a fairly new technology, errors and updates will occur more frequently. As a result, this book may tend to become out of date faster than a book about a more mature technology. But the basics will remain the same.

What this book is not about

This book is not a comprehensive look into the depths of Caché Objects, Atelier, and Eclipse. These three software applications are extremely sophisticated and complex and are not easily mastered.

This book, combined with the excellent InterSystems documentation as well as the Atelier and Eclipse documentation will give you a good starting point to learn and eventually master these software applications.

Interactive environments

Since Eclipse and Atelier both are interactive, which means that often menu items, functions, and options often appear and may disappear depending upon what you are working on, you may find items in this book may or may not always be present, it is easy to become confused. This will only be cured with time, knowledge and practice.

Where to Start

You want to learn much about the ins and outs of Atelier, go through chapters 5 through 8.

You want to learn about Caché and Atelier Routines, go through chapters 10 and 11.

You want to learn about Caché and Atelier Classes, go through chapters 12 through 17.

You want to learn about Object Technology, go through chapters, 9, 19, 20, and 21.

You want to learn a general background on Classes, chapter 18.

For other situations read the summary of chapters below and then decide on your best course of action.

Summary

Summary of the chapters.

Chapter 1 Overview

Purpose, what this book is not about, where to start, a brief overview of each chapter, highlights, my impressions, documentation, server-side development video, helpful hints: bookmarks, cheat sheets, help on search scope and tips and tricks, quick access box, note about Atelier/Eclipse editor as well as setup summary.

Chapter 2 When you need help

A listing of resources available when you need help understanding this technology. InterSystems Worldwide Support Center, InterSystems Developer Community, InterSystems Cube

Documentation, Web Browser, Website and Product Website Documentation, Atelier and Eclipse Documentation.

Chapter 3 General Introductions

Brief introductions into Caché, Caché Objects, Caché ObjectScript, MUMPS, Eclipse, IDE, and Atelier.

Chapter 4 Installations

How to install Java, Eclipse, Atelier Plugin and Caché on your computer.

Chapter 5 Atelier Overview

Working directory, welcome page, IDE configuration settings and Overview that covers workbench basics, Eclipse Marketplace, team support with Git, using the welcome page, introductory documentation, print documentation, Atelier videos, how to migrate to Atelier IDE, using the help system screen. Atelier working sets, Atelier editor and Caché Studio and Configuring a server connection.

Chapter 6 Atelier Dropdown Menus

Much of Atelier's functions exist in the dropdown menus off of the Workbench. These may seem simple and straight forward, but often they are not. It is a benefit to be at least familiar with them. Atelier Dropdown Menus: File, Edit, Source, Navigate, Search, Project, Run, External Tools, Tools, Window, Perspective, Navigation, and Help. Two items in the dropdown menu that have a wealth of information, the Window dropdown menu and Preference.

Chapter 7 Atelier Concepts

Learning Atelier, Concepts, Workbench, Perspectives, Views, Views Stacks, Projects, Editors, Windows, Resources, Atelier Server Connections, Source Code Templates.

Chapter 8 The Workbench

Setting up a Workspace, Rearranging Views and Editors, Copying, renaming and moving, Comparing, Platform Tips and Tricks.

Chapter 9 Object Basics

Goals of Object Technology, Terms of Object Technology, invoking a Class Method, Invoking a Method and Other Object Methods

> Chapter 10 is for working with a Routine in Studio and chapters 12, 14, and 16 are for working with a Class in Studio.

Chapter 10 Caché Studio - Create a Routine SLastNameRoutine

In Caché Studio, create the Routine SLastNameRoutine, run the Routine and execute the debugger.

Chapter 12 Caché Studio - Create a Class SLastName.Person

In Caché Studio, create the Class SLastName.Person with a property and index. Add data to the property. Difference between a Class and an Object. Then Saving your Class.

Chapter 14 Add Properties Studio Class SLastName.Person

Add more properties to SLastName.Person with the populate method. Then displayed the Class and data with SQL.

Chapter 16 Add Method Studio Class SLastName.Person

Add an Instance Method and a Class Method to Studio Class SLastName.Person.

> Chapter 11 is for working with a Routine in Atelier and chapters 13, 15, and 17 are for working with a Class in Atelier

Chapter 11 Atelier - Create a Routine ALastNameRoutine

In Atelier, create the Routine ALastNameRoutine, run the Routine and execute the debugger.

Chapter 13 Atelier - Create a Class ALastName.Person

In Atelier, create the Project TeamA and then the Class ALastName.Person with a property and index. Add data to the property. Difference between a Class and an Object. Then Saving your Class.

Chapter 15 Add Properties Atelier Class ALastName.Person

Add more properties to ALastName.Person with the populate method. Then displayed the Class and data with SQL.

Chapter 17 Add Method Atelier Class ALastName.Person

Add an Instance Method and a Class Method to Atelier Class ALastName.Person.

Chapter 18 Class Members

A review of the various Class Members; Properties, Parameters, Instance Methods, Class Methods, Queries, Indices, SQL Triggers, Foreign Keys, Storage, Projections , and XData.

Chapter 19 Relationships: One to Many

An example of how Relationships are coded in Atelier.

Chapter 20 Processing Relationships

Chapter 21 Inheritance

An explanation of Object Technology Inheritance as well as an example of how it works in Atelier.

Appendix A – Migration to Atelier

Appendix B – Automatic Software Update

Appendix C – Export and Import

Appendix D – Atelier Terminal Plugin

Appendix E – Regenerate a clean Storage

Appendix F – Object Commands

Appendix G – Comments

Appendix H – Content Assist

Appendix I – MUMPS or Caché?

Appendix J – Lexicon

Appendix K – Methods of Translation

Highlights

Highlights are special items.

Help – see Chapter 2

For brief introductions on **Caché, Caché Objects, Caché ObjectScript, MUMPS, Eclipse, IDE and Atelier** see Chapter 3.

Atelier Dropdown Menus see Chapter 6.

Customize Perspective see pages 60, 61, 62.

Save your Perspective see page 63

Show Active Key bindings – Ctrl+Shift+L twice

Cheat Sheets see Page 20.

For **Caché Installation** see Chapter 4.

For **Atelier concepts** see Chapter 7.

Chapter 8 shows **The Workbench.**

The Basics of Object see Chapter 9.

Class Members are in Chapter 18.

Caché Relationships are demonstrated in Chapters 19 and 20.

Object Inheritance is shown in Chapter 21.

Use the *Terminal* **that comes with Studio.**

Content Assist, see Appendix H.

Mapping Globals – Brendan Bannon, Page 181.

My impressions

In learning Atelier as a plug-in to Eclipse has been much like a treasure hunt to me. Everything is not hard and fast, strike that, nothing is hard and fast, except maybe my intractable brain. In some ways it has been like the old video game Zelda, (yes, I did play Zelda) you need to click everywhere, you can never be sure when you will find an egg, or surprise, or for that matter a disappointment.

My advice, keep learning, never grow tired of it. Atelier/Eclipse is a dynamic environment and changes as you continue in it. Initially, it will not always make since, but as you learn more it will.

Documentation too simple?

I have been accused of writing documentation that is too simple.

Yes, that is probably true. I struggle with documentation all the time. I feel the beginner has enough of a problem without me adding to it and I don't want to further complicate it with complex documentation.

Everybody, and I mean everybody had to start sometime, had to ask the simple questions. And most of us still need to. I write for that person.

But as we master the simple we become better equipped to take on the more complex.

Atelier for Server-Side Development Video

There is one YouTube video that I found especially helpful, it is entitled *Atelier for Server-Side Development*, check it out:

https://www.youtube.com/results?search_query=Atelier+for+Server-Side+Development

https://tinyurl.com/y8jr6jz6

Helpful hints

Bookmarks

Bookmarks are a quick and simple way to see your resources that you use often.

To see your bookmarks, from the Workbench → Windows Dropdown Menu → Show View → Bookmarks while you are in a specific resource. If that does not work, look at the documentation Workbench → Help → Welcome → Overview →Introductory Documentation and search for Bookmarks.

To add a bookmark, use the Edit Dropdown Menu.

To delete a bookmark, right click on the bookmark while viewing the bookmark from Windows → Show View → Bookmarks.

Cheat Sheets

To see the available Cheat Sheets, Help → Cheat Sheet and the following display will come up.

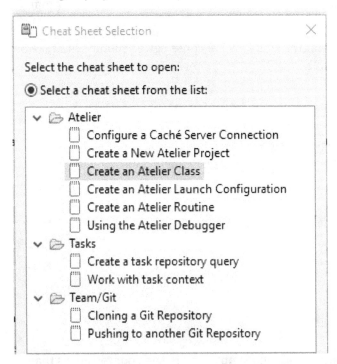

Help with Search – reduce your search scope

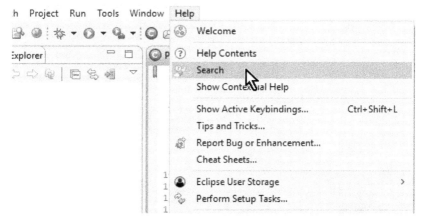

When you want help on "Search", (not Help Contents). This will bring up a screen that you can use to modify your Scope of the Search.

Click on Scope to change the scope of your search.

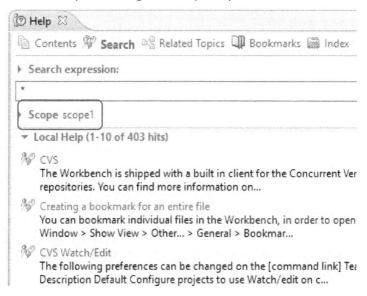

After you click on Scope then click on Advanced Settings and the screen on the left will come up so you can define your search scope.

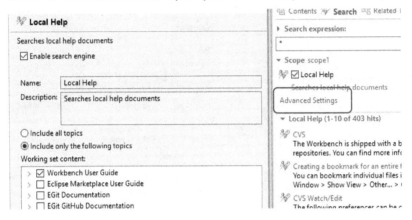

Also notice the other options available on the search screen.

- **Contents,**
- **Search,**
- **Related Topics,**
- **Bookmarks, and**
- **Index.**

Quick Access Box

There is one more item you need to see, on the right side of the screen is the *Quick Access box,* start typing any command in the box to search commands and see much more.

Note about Atelier/Eclipse Editor

The Atelier/Eclipse Class editor is much more involved and complicated than Studio. It takes considerable trial and error and practice to understand everything it has, and even then, there are more plugins to further complicate matters. But it is well worth the effort.

Setup Summary

There are a number of steps to be followed to begin working with Caché Objects and Atelier. You may have done some of them already but to be complete let me list them.

- ➢ Install Caché, version 2016.2 or higher
- ➢ Install Java, version 1.8 or higher.
- ➢ Install Eclipse
- ➢ Install Atelier plug-in into Eclipse
- ➢ Keep Atelier up-to-date

For more detail see *Chapter 4 Getting Started*

Everybody knows how to raise children,

except the people who have them.

P. J. O'Rourke.

Chapter 2 - When you need help

InterSystems Worldwide Support Center

> Support Center open 24/7/365.
>
> Telephone: +1 617 621–0700
>
> Fax: +1 617 374–9391
>
> Email: support@InterSystems.com
>
> Website: *http://www.InterSystems.com*
>
> Documentation: *http://doc.intersystems.com/*

InterSystems Developer Community

The *InterSystems Developer Community* is an online bulletin board where developers of InterSystems technology may come and ask questions, share code, and keep up-to-date. You need to be a member to post entries, becoming a member is free, just go to the website below and register.

A recent post, by an InterSystems instructor, in another group encourages developers to use the Developer Community for their questions. I believe InterSystems wants this to become the central hub for InterSystems developer activity.

Website: *https://community.intersystems.com/*

InterSystems Documentation, launched from the Caché Cube

Click on the small bluish Caché Cube (once you have installed Caché) in your system tray and select *Documentation*. A new window will open up in your default browser displaying the first page of Caché's online documentation. You can start there, or search for a subject, or search for "Using InterSystems Documentation."

There is a wealth of information in the online documentation.

- Spend some time looking around now and you will benefit later when searching for specific information.
- If all this is new, look for *Getting Started with Caché* on the first page of the *Documentation Home Page*.
- If you need generalized guidance type of information, look in the *Development Guides*.
- If you need specialized information, look in the *Development Reference*.
- There is also a section on *Caché Tutorials*.

Search the documentation:

The first page contains three different types of searches:

— <u>Search Box</u> on the right (not shown)

— $Ctrl-F$ search for searching the current Web Page

— And a more advanced Search. To invoke this search, click on *Search Page*.

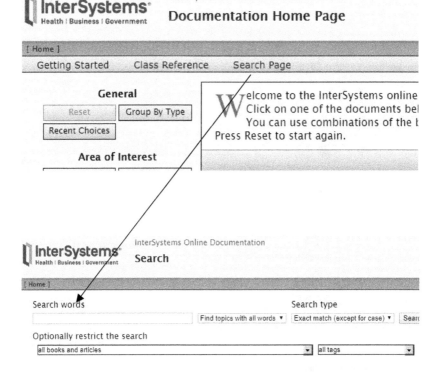

If you are new to InterSystems or Caché, you might find this helpful:

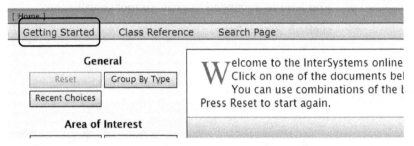

It will lead you to the following page:

InterSystems Online Documentation
Getting Started with Caché

[Home]

The material listed below will help you to get started using InterSystems products.

You can also go to the *Documentation Home Page*

FOR NEW CACHÉ USERS

- **Introduction to Caché** — An overview of Caché architecture and features.
- **Building Web Applications with Caché** — A tutorial that takes you through the steps of building an object-b
- **Basic System Administration** — A guide to administering your Caché System.
- **MultiValue and Caché** — Information on the MultiValue features of Caché.
- **Other Tutorial Offerings** — A map of the other tutorial offerings for self-paced learning.

FOR EXPERIENCED CACHÉ U:

- **Caché Release Notes** — A listing of the new features in this release.
- **Caché Upgrade Checklists** — A listing of changes in the release that may affect upgrades from earlier releases
- **Using Caché Studio** — Documentation for Caché Studio.
- **Caché Security Guide** — A description of the security features available with this version.

FOR ADDITIONAL INFORMATI

- **InterSystems Documentation** — A guide to finding and using information in online and PDF formats.
- **InterSystems Web Site** — Information about InterSystems Corporation and its products.
- **InterSystems Support** — Information about InterSystems Worldwide Response Center.
- **InterSystems Learning Services** — Information about our variety of training and certification programs.
- **Caché News Groups** — Discussion forums for Caché developers and users.

Documentation from the Web Browser

To access InterSystems' documentation without going through the Caché Cube, post this URL in your browser's address box

http://localhost:57772/csp/docbook/DocBook.csp

This assumes your Caché server is configured on port number 57772.

To find the Port Number (Web Server Port Number) on your system:

Click on the Caché Cube → Preferred Server → Add/Edit and you will see a table of Server Names and Web Server Ports.

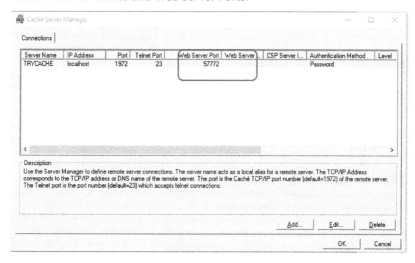

Documentation from InterSystems Website

To access InterSystems' documentation on the InterSystems Website as well as the PDF documentation files, post this URL in your browser's address box.

Website: *http://doc.intersystems.com/*

InterSystems Products Website

In addition, there is **much, much, more documentation** from InterSystem's products website *www.intersystems.com*

InterSystems Atelier Documentation

Website: *https://docs.intersystems.com/atelier/latest/index.jsp*

Eclipse Documentation

Website: *https://www.eclipse.org/documentation/*

Chapter 3 - General Introductions

What is Caché?

Caché (pronounced cash–shay, emphasis on the second syllable) is a product offered by InterSystems Corporation, Inc., *www.InterSystems.com*. InterSystems is a privately held software company based in Cambridge, Massachusetts USA founded in 1978. Caché is a *Multidimensional Data Server* integrated with its *Multidimensional Database*.

The *Caché Technology Guide* from InterSystems Inc. describes Caché as:

> *"Caché is a new generation of ultra–high–performance database technology. It combines an object database, high–performance SQL, and powerful Multidimensional data access – – all of which can simultaneously access the same data." –*
> *www.InterSystems.com*

What are Caché Objects?

The *Caché Technology Guide* from InterSystems Inc. describes the Caché Object model as:

> *Caché's object model (based upon the ODMG* standard) supports a full array of object programming concepts, including encapsulation, embedded objects, multiple inheritance, polymorphism, and collections.*
> *www.InterSystems.com*

*-see Glossary

Objects, or Object Technology is a new way to look at data processing. Simply put, an Object is data and the code that changes that data in one unit, or one object. In legacy applications, data was separated from the code that changed the data. By combining data and changes, we have a more complete, and manageable representation of the data. This should become clearer as you work through this book.

What is Caché ObjectScript?

Caché ObjectScript or "COS" is one of the programming languages used with Caché.

What is MUMPS?

MUMPS (Massachusetts General Hospital Utility Multi-Programming System), also known as M, is a general-purpose computer programming language that gives ACID (Atomic, Consistent, Isolated, and Durable) transaction processing. Its most unique and differentiating feature is its "built-in" database, enabling high-level access to disk storage using simple symbolic program variables and subscripted arrays, like the variables used by most languages to access main memory.

From its inception in the 1960s it has grown, been improved upon and serves as the basis for Caché which has grown from MUMPS.

Link to InterSystems Documentation

You can access InterSystems documentation either from the Caché Cube in your System Tray (after installing Caché, see Chapter 4) or from the hyperlink below.

Website: *http://doc.intersystems.com/*

What is Eclipse?

Eclipse is an Open source development platform which other modular software can "Plug-in" and run as part of Eclipse. It is an IDE.

Website: *https://www.eclipse.org/org/*

Website: *http://help.eclipse.org/oxygen/index.jsp?nav=%2F0*

What is an IDE?

An Integrated Development Environment (IDE) is a software application that provides comprehensive facilities to computer programmers for software development. An IDE normally consists of a source code editor, build automation tools and a debugger. Most modern IDEs have intelligent code completion.

--From Wikipedia

What is Atelier?

Atelier is InterSystems' Eclipse-based development environment. It enables you to rapidly build solutions that leverage the performance, scalability, connectivity, and reliability of the InterSystems Data Platform.

--From InterSystems

Website: *https://docs.intersystems.com/atelier/latest/index.jsp*

Atelier – background

An Atelier (French: [atəlje], "workshop" or "studio") is, in English, the private workshop or studio of a professional artist in the fine or decorative arts, where a principal master and a number of assistants, students, and apprentices can work together producing pieces of fine art or visual art released under the master's name or supervision.

This was the standard vocational practice for European artists from the Middle Ages to the 19th century, and common elsewhere in the world. In medieval Europe such a way of working and form of visual or fine art education was often enforced by local guild regulations, of the painters' Guild of Saint Luke, and those of other guilds for other crafts.

Apprentices usually began young, working on simple tasks, and after some years became journeymen, before becoming masters themselves. The system was gradually replaced as the once powerful guilds declined, and the academy became a favored method of training, although many professional artists continued to use students and assistants, some paid by the artist, some paying fees to learn.

--From Wikipedia

Chapter 4 – Installations

There are a number of steps to begin working with Java, Eclipse, Atelier, and Caché. You may have done some of them already but to be complete let me list them.

> Install Java, version 1.8 or higher.

1. To check if you already have Java installed, and if so what version enter this in an OS Terminal: *java –version*

For example, from a Windows Command Prompt

2. To install Java for the first time, a newer version of Java, or a different bitness of Java (Java bitness should match the Eclipse bitness) check this website: http://www.oracle.com/technetwork/java/javase/downloads/jdk8-downloads-2133151.html

> Install Eclipse
> Install Atelier plug-in into Eclipse
> Keep Atelier up-to-date – see Appendix B
> Install Caché, version 2016.2 or higher – see below

Please note, Atelier is available only as an Eclipse plugin.

Install Eclipse and Atelier as a Plugin

InterSystems put together a good document on how to install Eclipse and Atelier I direct your attention to it.

Website: *https://community.intersystems.com/post/announcement-atelier-only-available-eclipse-plugin*

If you have any trouble with the above, you can report it on the InterSystems Developer Community.

Website: *https://community.intersystems.com/*

Atelier Development Environment

I have been trying to understand the Atelier Development Environment with all the dropdown menus and various Perspectives and Views.

I find it all confusing. What comes to mind is an old rubber tire that has so many patches on it that there are more patches than tire.

Another thought on the Atelier Develop Environment is an old time Labyrinth with all the various paths to follow without knowing where they lead.

Medieval labyrinth.

The Atelier Development Environment is like the old time Zelda video games, **you click on everything.**

Notwithstanding my criticism of the Atelier Development Environment, nestled within Eclipse, it does seem to work and work very well, for the most part. As long as you can grasp the complexity of it all.

I will try to direct you through this maze, or at least the parts I find significant and the parts that carry out the goal of understanding Object Technology and creating Object Classes.

Eclipse Market Place

There are many Eclipse Aftermarket plug-ins available. Whether they all work as advertised or not is up to you to discover. And especially whether they work with Atelier. In time I have no doubt that our own people will create plug-ins that directly improve Atelier. I would love to see this product 5 years from now.

Website: *https://marketplace.eclipse.org/*

Installing Caché

InterSystems Inc. allows you to download a single copy of Caché to your own computer at no cost. This is available from *www.InterSystems.com*.

Open the link *https://download.intersystems.com/download/register.csp* and follow the instructions to register yourself or sign in if you already have an account. Follow the instructions on how to download and install Caché.

After you have downloaded the Caché install file, double click on the executable file, and let it run taking the default answers for all the questions. You will be asked for a user name and password, remember these, you will need them later.

Having Caché on your own computer will help immeasurably as you read this book and work the examples.

The Caché Cube

Once the installation is complete, a small cube will appear in your system tray. Click on it and you will see the following menu:

Figure 1 The Caché Cube

The Caché Startup Menu

- ➢ Getting Started
- ➢ Start Caché – start the Caché Instance
- ➢ Stop Caché – stop the Caché Instance
- ➢ Studio – platform upon which to develop your software
- ➢ Terminal – platform upon which to run your software
- ➢ Management Portal – numerous items for managing the Caché Instance
- ➢ Documentation
- ➢ Remote System Access – accessing a system remotely
- ➢ Preferred Server
- ➢ About
- ➢ Exit

Chapter 5 – Atelier Overview

All editing done locally

Before we begin, one difference between Atelier and Caché Studio needs to be noted. All Routines and Classes must be associated with a local project, and, all projects are local. It is only when you save the Class or Routine that it will be saved to the server. This is different than Caché Studio. With Caché Studio you work on the Class or Routine that is on the server.

Workspace Directory

To get started, click on the Eclipse Shortcut, you will be presented with the following display. This is your working or workspace directory. You may have as many working directories as you need. Your working directory remembers where you are and will return you there the next time you enter.

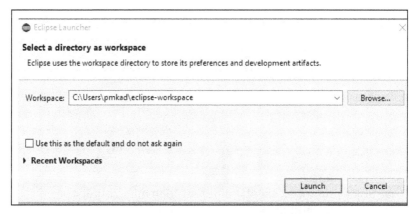

Notice the box you can click on to use this as a default and you will not be asked again. Also, as you use more directories the recent ones will be displayed.

This display is important, because if you need to start over all you will need to do is exit, change the name of your workspace, and restart. Later you should go back and clean up the unused workspace files.

There will be times while in Eclipse/Atelier you may not know how to proceed and cannot seem to go back, at these times it will be helpful to just start over.

Welcome Page

If Eclipse does not start on this welcome page, I would suggest to click on *Help* → *Welcome* page.

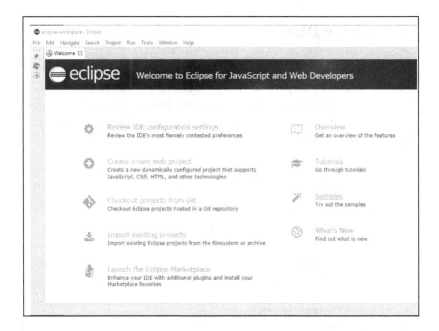

Your display may look slightly different than mine, but it does not matter as long as all the elements are there.

Review IDE configuration settings

I suggest you go through and *Review the IDE configuration settings*, click on the check marks if you want a specific setting. Many of the settings you may want.

Overview

Now click on *Overview* and the following screen will come up.

We will look at the various items on this screen.

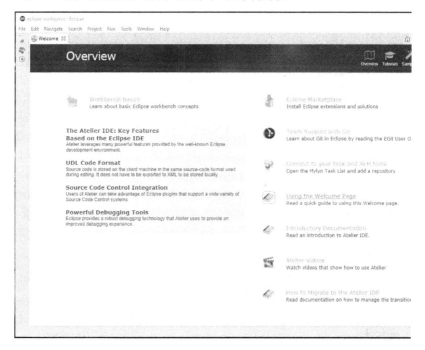

Workbench Basics

This item contains good information about the Workbench, which is your desktop environment. Much of your time will be spent in the Workbench.

From the Overview screen

Eclipse Marketplace

Eclipse Marketplace will present you with various items or plug-ins you can install. From what I have seen there are tools on an image editor, housekeeping, more Java support, arbitrary lines in your files, collaboration tools, Red Hat, etc. The one I am looking for but have not found is key board macros.

Team Support with Git.

Good stuff especially if you are involved in Git.

Using the Welcome Page

I recommend you go through this presentation.

Introductory Documentation

The Eclipse/Atelier documentation is fairly good, however in many ways it is a shot-gun approach, all this information flies at you, you need to run around trying to catch it all and then you are expected to put it in some sort of order, not an easy task.

There are some good ideas, like the Cheat-Sheet concept, which steps you through a task. But do not rely too heavily on the Cheat-Sheets or you will not learn to do it on your own.

Do not use this book exclusively, use it in conjunction with the InterSystems documentation. As I said before this is a "Getting Started" type of book, not a comprehensive manual.

> From the Overview screen

Print the Documentation

You may want to print the entire set of documentation, it will take a good amount of paper, but you may find it useful. From the *Overview* you will see *Introductory Documentation.*

Atelier Videos

These are videos produced by InterSystems Community Development. You will need to log into the Community Development Website.

Website: *https://community.intersystems.com/*

How to Migrate to Atelier IDE

Good detailed documentation on how to move your code to Atelier

Now from the Overview top right of the page we have.

Tutorials

Atelier IDE Tutorials

Using the Help System Screen

From the Overview screen

This is from the Overview screen or Help → Help Contents.

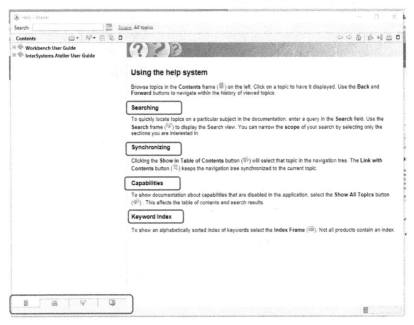

This screen talks about **Searching, Synchronizing, Capabilities**, and **Keyword Index**. At the bottom of the *content window* are four icons,

1) Contents,
2) Index,
3) Search Results, and
4) Bookmarks

If you hover over the icons, you can identify which is which.

This screen also shows various buttons, see the rectangles above.

You should spend some time with this screen to get a good understanding of how it works. It is not as simple and straight-forward as one might think and has some very helpful and interesting features.

What's New

New Software Updates – if you do not have auto updates turned on you should visit this menu item on a regular basis. Also see Appendix B.

Eclipse Community

Just as the InterSystems Developer Community helps those developers for InterSystems, the Eclipse Community does so for those interested in Eclipse.

Website: *http://www.eclipse.org/*

Atelier Working sets

As I understand this concept, your *Working set* is a number of adjustments that change depending upon what you are working on. In other words, the system knows what you are doing and applies your predefined preferences.

For example, if you set up a number of break points for a certain routine, whenever you are in that routine you will always have those break points.

Following is a screen shot on how the documentation defines it.

From your *Workbench* → *Help dropdown menu* → *Help Contents* → *Search for: Working sets*

Atelier Editor and Caché Studio

Is Atelier better than Caché Studio? I would say yes, but then there is this learning curve with Atelier, but that is true with all new software.

In its wisdom, InterSystems has chosen to go with Atelier so we have no choice. At some point in the future Caché Studio will disappear. It is better to bite the bullet now and learn it sooner rather than later.

Configuring a Server Connection

When you first come into Atelier you may need to set up your Connection Configuration. What that means is to ensure that Atelier and Caché can talk to each other. From your *Workbench → Help dropdown menu → Help Contents → Search for: Configuring a Server Connection.*

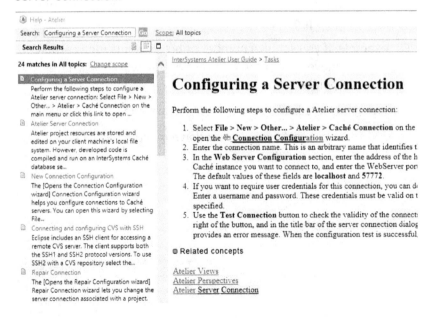

Chapter 6 – Atelier Dropdown Menus

Atelier Dropdown Menus

Much of Atelier's functions exist in the dropdown menus off of the Workbench. These may seem simple and straight forward, but often they are not. Several items in the dropdown menu that have a wealth of information, the **Window dropdown menu with Perspective and Preference.**

File dropdown menu

- ➢ New Alt+Shift+N
  Atelier Projects, Projects, Custom File, Routine File, Class File, CSP File, Example . . . , Other . . . Ctrl+N
- ➢ Open File – this opens any file on your directory
- ➢ Open Projects from File System
- ➢ Close Ctrl+W
- ➢ Close All Ctrl+Shift+W
- ➢ Save Ctrl+S
- ➢ Save As
- ➢ Save All Ctrl+Shift+S
- ➢ Revert – revert or roll back you changes
- ➢ Move
- ➢ Rename F2
- ➢ Refresh F5
- ➢ Convert line Delimiters to Windows
- ➢ Convert line Delimiters to Unix

Reviewing Atelier dropdown menus: File dropdown menu

- ➤ Import – using one of the Import Wizards, you can Import Archive Files, Breakpoints, Classes, Configurations, Elements, File Systems, Git data, Launch Tasks, Preferences Projects, XML Script, and XML Data
- ➤ Export – using one of the Export Wizards, you can Import Archive Files, Breakpoints, Classes, Configurations, Elements, File Systems, Git data, Launch Tasks, Preferences Projects, XML Script, and XML Data.
- ➤ Properties – displays properties for the Class or whatever resource is selected – Alt+Enter – Display resources.
- ➤ Switch Workspace – option to switch to another Workspace and copy your settings.
- ➤ Restart

Edit dropdown menu

- ➤ Undo – Ctrl+Z
- ➤ Redo – Ctrl+Y
- ➤ Cut – Ctrl+X
- ➤ Copy – Ctrl+C
- ➤ Paste – Ctrl+V
- ➤ Delete - Delete
- ➤ Select All – Ctrl+A
- ➤ Toggle Block Selection – Alt+Shift+A
- ➤ Find and Replace – Ctrl+F
- ➤ Find Next – Ctrl+K
- ➤ Find Previous – Ctrl+Shift+K
- ➤ Incremental Find Next Ctrl+J

Reviewing Atelier dropdown menus: Edit dropdown menu

- ➤ Incremental Find Previous - Ctrl+Shift+J
- ➤ Add Bookmark – add a Bookmark name
- ➤ Add Task – add a new Task
- ➤ Smart Insert Mode – Ctrl+Shift+Insert
- ➤ Show Tool Tip description – F2
- ➤ Content Assist – default Ctrl+Space - See Appendix H
- ➤ Parameter Hints – Ctrl+Shift+Space
- ➤ Word Completion – Alt+/ - This action will attempt to complete the word currently being entered.
- ➤ Quick Fix – Ctrl+1
- ➤ Set encoding

Source dropdown menu

- ➤ Toggle Comment – Ctrl+/ – make the selected line into a comment
- ➤ Comment – make the selected line a comment
- ➤ Uncomment – remove the selected line as a comment
- ➤ Shift Left – shift the selected line one tab to the left
- ➤ Shift right – shift the selection line one tab to the right

Navigate dropdown menu

- ➤ Go Into – used in Debug
- ➤ Goto
  - ○ Back
  - ○ Forward
  - ○ Up One Level

Reviewing Atelier dropdown menus: Navigate dropdown menu

- o Previous Member – Ctrl+Shift+Up
- o Next Member – Ctrl+Shift+Down
- o Matching Bracket Ctrl+Shift+P
➢ Open Atelier Class/Routine – Ctrl+Shift+T
➢ Open Task – Ctrl+F12
➢ Activate Task – Ctrl+F9
➢ Deactivate Task – Ctrl+Shift+F9
➢ Open Setup for
    User/Installation/Workspace/Eclipse.org/Parent Models
➢ Open Setup Log
➢ Show in – Alt+Shift+W for
  - o Atelier Explorer
  - o Terminal
  - o Script Explorer
  - o Outline
  - o System Explorer
  - o Properties
➢ Quick Outline Ctrl+O
➢ Next Annotation – Ctrl+Shift+.
➢ Previous Annotation – Ctrl+Shift+,
➢ Last Edit Location – Ctrl+Q
➢ Goto Line Ctrl+L
➢ Back – Alt+<
➢ Forward – Alt+>

Search dropdown menu

Search – Ctrl+H – brings up this display.

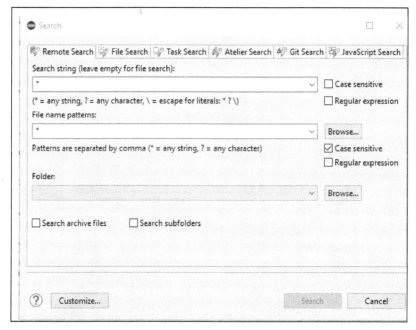

Notice the tabs at the top of this display:

- **Remote Search**
- **File Search**
- **Task Search**
- **Atelier Search**
- **Git Search**
- **Java Search**

This screen also allows, you to search archive files and subfolders and there is even a *Customize* button for search categories.

Since this is an introductory book, I won't go into detail on this search screen, but it is obvious that it is extensive.

Now continuing with the search dropdown menu.

Reviewing Atelier dropdown menus: Search dropdown menu

- ➢ File
- ➢ Remote
- ➢ Text –
    - ○ Workspace – Ctrl+Alt+G
    - ○ Project
    - ○ File
    - ○ Working Set

Project dropdown menu

- ➢ Open Project
- ➢ Close Project
- ➢ Build All – Ctrl+B
- ➢ Build Project
- ➢ Build Working Set
- ➢ Clean
- ➢ Build Automatically
- ➢ Compile Configuration
- ➢ Synchronize Ctrl+Alt+S
- ➢ Properties

Run dropdown menu

- ➢ Run – Ctrl+F11
- ➢ Debug – F11
- ➢ Run History
- ➢ Run As
- ➢ Run Configurations – brings up this display

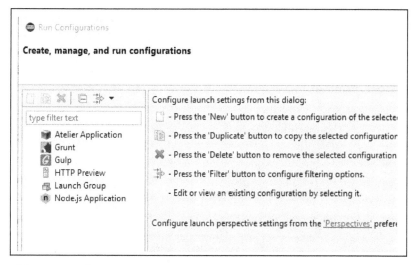

This screen allows you to Create, Manage and Run a number of configurations, namely; Atelier Application, Grunt, Gulp, HTTP Preview, Launch Group, and Node.js Application.

Now continuing with the run, or debug dropdown menu.

> ➢ Debug History
> ➢ Debug As
> ➢ Debug Configuration – brings up this display.

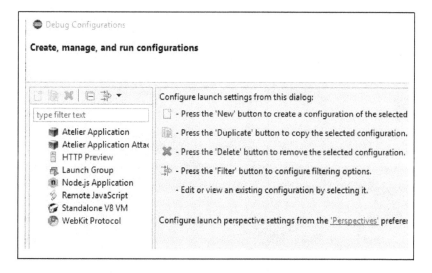

The prior screen is similar to the one preceding it, but instead of running configurations it allows you to debug configurations.

Now continuing with the debug dropdown menu.

➤ External Tools

    ○ Run As

    ○ External Tools Configuration – brings up this display.

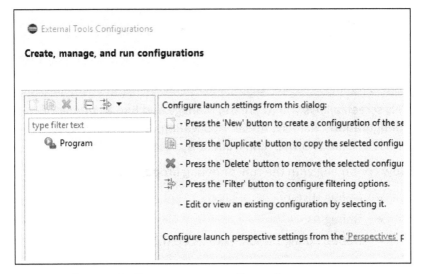

Again, we have a similar screen on configurations.

Now continuing with the External Tools and Tools

    ○ Organize Favorites

Tools dropdown menu

> ➤ Add-ins – brings up the following display on selecting a project.

> ➤ Templates.

Window dropdown menu

The Window dropdown menu is one of the most complicated menus and full of functions.

> ➤ New Window – bring up a new window.
> ➤ Editor
>> ○ Toggle Split Editor – (Horizontal) Ctrl + _
>> ○ Toggle Split Editor – (Vertical) Ctrl + {
>> ○ Clone
>> ○ Toggle Word Wrap

Reviewing Atelier dropdown menus: Window dropdown menu

- o Show whitespace Characters
- o Zoom in – Ctrl++
- o Zoom out – Ctrl+-
- ➢ Appearance
  - o Hide Toolbar
  - o Hide Status Bar
  - o Toggle Full Screen – Alt+F11
  - o Maximize Active View or Editor – Ctrl+M
  - o Minimize Active View or Editor
- ➢ Show View
  - o Atelier Explorer
  - o Bookmark
  - o Console – Alt+Shift Q,C
  - o Error Log - Alt+Shift Q,L
  - o Outline - Alt+Shift Q,O
  - o Project Explorer
  - o Properties
  - o Server Explorer
  - o Other . . .

    Note: it seems like once an item is selected from Other, it is moved up to a higher menu

- ➢ Perspective

  The Perspective has many options that control your environment.

  However, keep in mind that Atelier itself is classified as a Perspective.

  - o Open Perspective

Reviewing Atelier dropdown menus: Window dropdown menu:
Perspective

- o Customized Perspective - definition
  Each Workbench window has one or more
  perspectives. A perspective defines the first set and
  layout of views in the Workbench window. Within
  each of the windows, each perspective shares the
  same set of editors. Each perspective provides a set
  of functions aimed at carrying out a specific task or
  type of task or works with specific types of
  resources. Perspectives control what appears in
  certain menus and toolbars. They define the visible
  action sets, which you can change to customize a
  perspective. You can save a perspective that you
  build in this manner, making your own custom
  perspective.
- o Customized Perspective – brings up this window
  with 4 tags:
  - – Tool Bar Visibility
  - – Menu Visibility
  - – Action Set Availability
  - – Shortcuts

Reviewing Atelier dropdown menus: Window dropdown menu:
Customize Perspective

⬤ Customize Perspective - Atelier

| Tool Bar Visibility | Menu Visibility | Action Set Availability | Shortcuts |

Choose which tool bar items to display.

Tool Bar Structure:

Find the four full displays on the next two pages.

- — Tool Bar Visibility
- — Menu Visibility
- — Action Set Availability
- — Shortcuts

Please notice all the items these 4 screens control.

- — **The first screen controls the <u>Tool Bar Visibility</u>**
- — **The second screen controls the <u>Menu Visibility</u>**
- — **The third screen controls the <u>Action Set Visibility</u>**
- — **The fourth screen controls the <u>Short Cuts</u>**

As you can see, with these four control screens you have complete control over your custom perspective.

This is obviously more advanced than I can cover in this book, but I just wanted to give you a taste of what can be done with a custom perspective.

Customize Perspective – Atelier - <u>Tool Bar Visibility</u>

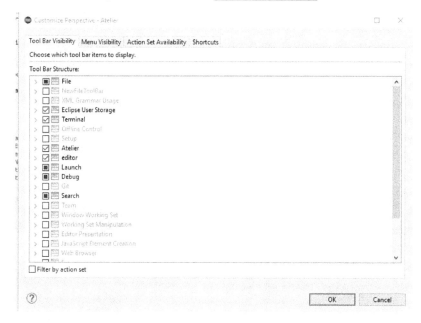

Customize Perspective – Atelier - <u>Menu Visibility</u>

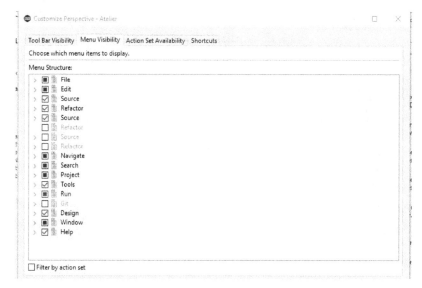

Customize Perspective – Atelier – <u>Action Set Availability</u>

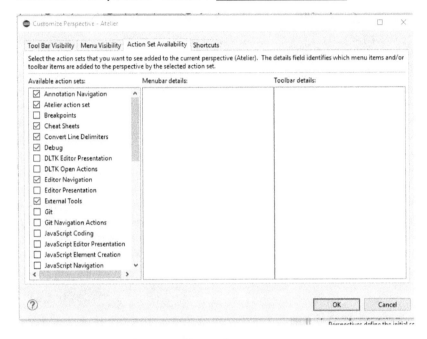

Customize Perspective – Atelier – <u>Shortcuts</u>

Reviewing Atelier dropdown menus: Window dropdown menu:
Perspective

Save Perspective As – brings up this display. These are the current
Perspectives available for this instance of Eclipse. Typically, you
would save Perspective as Atelier.

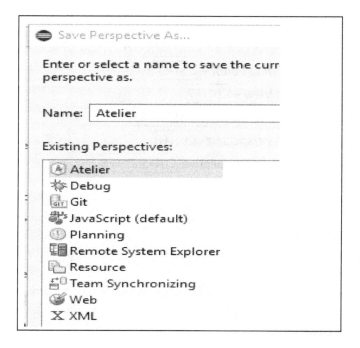

- o   Reset Perspective
- o   Close/Close All

> Reviewing Atelier dropdown menus: Window dropdown menu

- ➢ Navigation
  - o Show System Menu – Alt+-
  - o Show View Menu – Ctrl+F10
  - o Quick Access – Ctrl+3
  - o Activate Editor – F12
  - o Next Editor – Ctrl+F6
  - o Previous Editor – Ctrl+Shift+F6
  - o Switch to Editor – Ctrl+Shift+E
  - o Next View – Ctrl+F7
  - o Previous View – Ctrl+Shift+F7
  - o Next Perspective- Ctrl+F8
  - o Previous Perspective-Ctrl+Shift+F8

Preferences

Within Preferences is a wealth of information and settings.

You can access your Preferences from the Windows dropdown menu. Another way to bring up your Preferences is to hit Ctrl+Shift+L twice.

Following are item I consider significant within Preferences.

- • General
  - o Appearance – defines how Eclipse looks
  - o Content Types
  - o Editors – autosave and file associations along with Text Editor specifications
  - o Error Reporting – set defaults for error reporting

Reviewing Atelier dropdown menus: Window dropdown menu-
Preferences

- o **Keys – with this option you can output a listing of all 300+ keys along with their commands and descriptions used within Eclipse**
- o Network connections
- o Notifications
- o Perspectives available
- o Search
- o Startup and Shutdown
- o Web browser
- o Welcome
- o Workspace - specifications
- Atelier
  - o Caching
  - o Colors
  - o Compilation
  - o Connection
  - o Debug
  - o Editors
  - o Save Settings
  - o Templates
  - o Validation

- Dynamic Languages
  - o Validators
- Help
  - o Content
- Install/Update
  - o Automatic Updates
  - o Available Software Sites

Reviewing Atelier dropdown menus: Window dropdown menu-
Preferences

- JavaScript
  - o Appearance
  - o Code Style
  - o Debug
  - o Editor
  - o Include Path
  - o Runtimes
  - o Validator
- JSON
- Oomph
- Remote Systems
  - o DataStore
  - o File Caché
  - o Files
  - o Logging
  - o Passwords
  - o SSL
- Run/Debug
  - o Console
  - o External Tools
  - o Launching
  - o Perspectives
  - o String Substitution
  - o TCP/IP Monitor
  - o View Management
- Server
- Team
  - o File Content
  - o Git

Reviewing Atelier dropdown menus: Window dropdown menu-
Preferences

- o   Ignored Resources
- o   Models
- Terminal
- Web
- XML
  - o   DTD Files
  - o   XML Catalog
  - o   XML Files
  - o   XML Schema Files

Help dropdown menu

- ➢   Welcome – brings you to the front-end screen.
- ➢   Help Contents – brings you to the top-level help screen to begin a search.
- ➢   Search – brings you to the search screen on the current level.
- ➢   Show Contextual Help
- ➢   **Show Active Key bindings – Ctrl+Shift+L - opens a small window of key bindings, type Ctrl+Shift+L again and you will be put in a Preference window with all the 300+ Key bindings.**
- ➢   Tips and Tricks
- ➢   Report bug or enhancements – this is a way of sending information to the Eclipse Development Community.
- ➢   Cheat Sheets – the following will be displayed.

Reviewing Atelier dropdown menus: Help menu

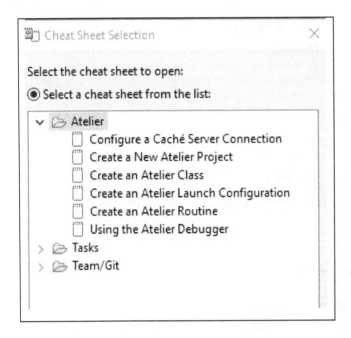

> Eclipse User Storage
> Perform Setup Tasks
> Check for Updates
> Install New Software
> Eclipse Market Place
> About Eclipse

Chapter 7 - Atelier Concepts

Learning Atelier

Atelier is easy to learn, and Atelier is hard to learn.

Much is familiar, and much is not.

I am not being facetious here, there are parts of Atelier that are simple and straight forward, and then there are other parts that are not so straight forward nor simple.

At the root of this is Eclipse. Much of Atelier is based on Eclipse. If you do well with Eclipse, you will do well with Atelier. And if you know little about Eclipse, then Atelier will be much more difficult.

Either way, it must be done.

Atelier Concepts

If you find some of these Concepts difficult, you are not alone.

So much seems to be crammed into the GUI display it is very easy to tie yourself into knots just trying to get around. It would be nice for InterSystems to produce an outline or some sort of map.

Plan on spending some quality time with Atelier and their concepts, there is no easy way around it.

To my way of thinking, concepts should be simple, straight forward and easy to understand.

Or so I thought. As I started to look at the concepts in the documentation, well, not so much.

In the Atelier documentation there are differing and often confusing information as far as the concepts. The following is just a guide, do not judge me too harshly if my interpretation of these concepts differs from yours.

In addition to reading these pages on concepts, I highly recommend you read the Atelier documentation of the same.

To see the Concepts from the Atelier documentation,

From the *Workbench → Help → Welcome → Overview →
Introductory Documentation and then the Concepts.*

I will not cover all the Concepts listed but those I thought more important. In reviewing the list of Concepts, you may however think other Concepts are important. The list of Concepts is on the next page and I encourage you to review the list.

Also, I added some items I thought should be in the concepts.

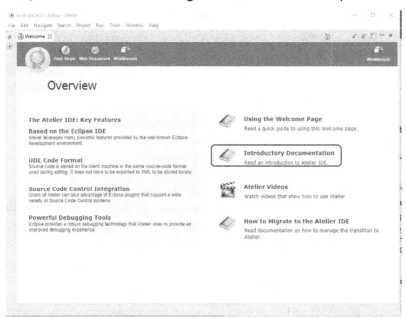

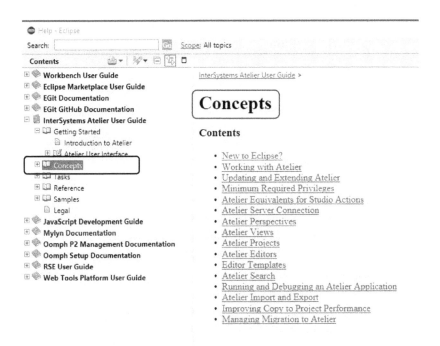

Workbench

Your Workbench is simply your desktop environment. A Workbench is subdivided into Perspectives, and with Perspectives there are Views, Editors, Projects, and Windows.

Perspectives

Perspectives are designed for working with Atelier projects. It is a collection of views and editors designed to perform a specific set of tasks. I like to think of Perspectives as environments.

There is a specific Perspective for Atelier and I encourage you to use it until you have gained enough knowledge to think otherwise.

To set your Perspective to Atelier, from you *Workbench* → *Window* → *Perspective* → *Open Perspective* → *Atelier*.

Views

Views encompass and support editors, presentations, menus, toolbars and buttons.

View Stacks

A View Stack is a number of views grouped together on the Workbench. You can select which View you wish to see from the Stack.

Projects

An Atelier project is the top-level container of all the source files and related resources for an application or feature. All Atelier resources must be part of a project. You cannot modify any resources unless it is in a Project and a Project must be local.

A project is stored as a directory in your workspace, which is on your client machine's <u>local</u> file system. Note that the Project is in your local file system, not on the server environment. This is different from Caché Studio.

Editors

Multiple editor types are provided depending upon the file type being edited.

➤ Atelier Class Editor (.cls)
➤ Atelier INC Editor Include files (.inc)
➤ Atelier INT Editor Intermediate files (.int)
➤ Atelier MAC Editor Routine source files. (.mac)
➤ Atelier Web Editor (.cls, .js, .htm, .html, .shtml)
➤ Atelier BPL Editor Diagram editor for Ensemble Business Process Language (BPL) or Data Transformation Language (DTL).

Windows

Windows allow you to hide, display or manipulate the views, perspectives, and actions in the Workbench.

Resources

Resources are a term used that includes multiple projects, *views, editors, files, folders, etc. in the Workbench.*

Atelier Server Connection

Resources for Atelier projects are stored and edited on your client's machine. But code is compiled and run on the Caché database server instance. Because of this every Atelier project needs to be associated with a Caché database server instance, or *Server Connection.*

Required properties include: Connection Name, Web Server Address and Port and may also require a user name and password.

Source Code Templates

The Atelier class editor provides various templates for frequently-used patterns. Templates are structured patterns. You insert a template by typing the CTRL+Space with your content assist keystrokes.

Chapter 8 - The Atelier Workbench

The Workbench is your desktop environment. It is where your projects are broken down into Classes and Routines and the other resources.

To support Classes and Routines, as well as the other elements, a Workbench employs Perspectives, Views, Editors, Windows, Files, and Folders. All of which are collectively called: *Resources*. A major part of developers' work is carried out in the Workbench and understanding the elements is necessary.

Items briefly covered in this chapter are:

- Setting up a Workspace,
- Rearranging Views and Editors,
- Copying, Renaming, and Moving,
- Comparing, and
- Platform Tips and Tricks

Setting up a Workspace

In setting up your workspace you need to be concerned with:

- Line Endings, and
- Text File Encoding.

Before you do anything, set your perspective to Atelier.

From the *Workbench* → *Windows* → *Perspective* → *Open Perspective* → *Atelier*.

Setting up a Workbench

The following documentation walks you through setting up your Workbench.

From the *Workbench* → *Help* → *Help Contents* → *Search for* → *Setting up the Workspace*

Rearranging Views and Editors

From the *Workbench* → *Help* → *Help Contents* → *Search for* → *Rearranging Views and Editors*

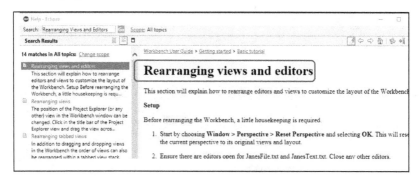

Copying, renaming, and moving

Workbench resources may be copied, renamed and moved depending upon your requirements.

See the following documentation.

From the *Workbench* → *Help* → *Help Contents* → *Search for* → *Copying, renaming and moving*

Comparing Resources

In the Workbench you can compare a number of resources and present the results in a special editor.

See the following documentation.

From the *Workbench* → *Help* → *Help Contents* → *Search for* → *Comparing resources.*

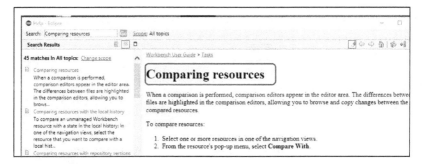

Platform Tips and Tricks

This is perhaps one of the most useful help items in the entire help file, the Platform Tips and Tricks.

See the following documentation.

From the *Workbench* → *Help* → *Help Contents* → *Search for* → *Platform Tips and Tricks*.

I will list what I think are some of the more significant items starting on the next page.

Many of the items are summarized, if you do not understand what is in this book go to the Eclipse/Atelier explanations.

The Tips and Tricks are broken down into the following sub-headings:

- – Workbench
- – Editing
- – Help

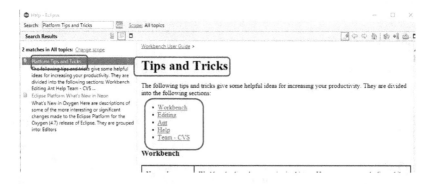

Here is a subject listing of the Workbench Tips and Tricks. You will need to go into Eclipse/Atelier to see exactly how they work.

Not all Tip and Tricks are covered in this list.

Workbench Tips and Tricks

- **Now, where was I** - Workbench editors keep a history. If you open a second editor while you're editing, you can press *Navigate* → *Backward* (*Alt+Left Arrow*, or the ◁▾ back arrow on the workbench toolbar) to go back to the last editor.
- **Quick access** - You can quickly find user interface elements with the *Quick Access* search box at the top right of the workbench window. Click in this field. Matching elements include open editors, perspectives, views, preferences, wizards, and commands. Start typing the name of the item you wish to find.
- **Quick access as a popup** - If the *Quick Access* field takes up too much space, you can hide it by selecting *Hide* from the context menu in the toolbar. Once hidden, pressing *Ctrl+3* will show a popup dialog.

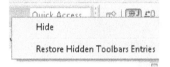

- **Full Screen mode** - You can toggle full screen mode with a shortcut (*Alt+F11*).
- **Ctrl+E** - opens a list of all open editors.
- **Automatic Save** – in the *Windows dropdown menu* → *Preference* → *General* → *Editors* → *Autosave* preference page you can enable or disable the autosave. In addition, you can change the time interval of autosave.
- **OLE** (Object Linking and Embedding), **editors** - By default Microsoft Word or Excel open as in-place editors inside of Eclipse. You can force these applications to open as stand-alone applications by unchecking the "Allow in-place system editors" option on the *Windows dropdown menu* → *Preference* → *General* → *Editors preference page*.
- **Opening editors with drag and drop** - You can open an editor by dragging an item from a view like the Project Explorer or Package Explorer and dropping it over the editor.

Workbench Tips and Tricks - continued

- **Tiling an editors' work area** - use drag and drop to change the layout of the editors' work area. Grasp an editor or view tab and drag it to the edge of the editor's work area and the work area will split.
- **Splitting an editor** – To view or edit multiple sections of an editor at once, you can split / unsplit the currently active editor via:
  - *Window dropdown menu* → *Editor* → *Toggle Split Editor (Horizontal)*
  - *Window dropdown menu* → *Editor* → *Toggle Split Editor (Vertical)*
- **Cloning an Editor** – From the *Windows dropdown menu* → *Editor* → *Clone*
- **Single click mode** - From the *Windows dropdown menu* → *General Preference page* you can activate single click opening for editors.
- **Collapsing all Button** - Use the Collapse all button in the Project Explorer view, and other views to collapse all expanded projects and folder items.

- **Global find/replace** – from the Search dropdown menu, select *file* and the following display will come up. Enter what you want to find/replace Then press *Replace*.

You can see all the options available on the Search screen above. I Encourage you to experiment with them.

Workbench Tips and Tricks - continued

- **Show in System Explorer** – When you right click on a resource, you see *Show In* → *System Explorer* context menu entry. This will open the folder with that resource in your system's explorer.

- **Linking view to current open editor** - The Project Explorer view, as well as other views may not be tightly linked with the current open editor. This means that closing or switching editors may not change the selection in the Project Explorer view. By selecting the *Link with Editor* button in the Project Explorer view toolbar ties the view to always show the current file being edited.

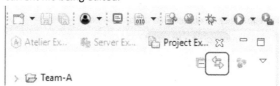

- **Manual editor / view synchronization** - The *Windows dropdown menu* → *Navigation* → *Show In* command gives a uniform way to navigate from an open editor to a view showing a corresponding file, or from a file selected in one view to the same file in a different view.
  Typing *Alt+Shift+W* opens a shortcut menu with the available view targets.

- **Quick navigation between views, editors and perspectives** -
  The *Window dropdown menu* → *Navigation* shows a number of ways to quickly navigate between the various resources.

- **Switch editors and multi-page editors**
  You can use *Ctrl+PageDown* to activate the next editor tab.
  Ctrl+PageUp to activate the previous editor tab, even in multi-page editors.

Workbench Tips and Tricks - continued

- **Minimizing views and editors** – You can maximize a view or editor by double-clicking on the view's title bar or the editor's tab. Double-click again to restore it to its usual size.
- **Detached views and editors** - You can detach a view or editor so that it can be placed wherever you want it, including over another Eclipse window. Drag the view by its tab to a location outside the workbench to detach it. You can also drag and drop other views into the same window.
- **Restoring a perspective's layout** – To restore or reset a perspective's layout: *Window download menu* → *Perspective* → *Reset Perspective.*
- **Customizable key bindings** – To customize keys, go to *Window download menu* → *Preference* → General → *Keys.*
- **All keyboard shortcuts** – To get a listing of all keyboard shortcuts hit *Ctrl-Shift-L twice*.
- **Key binding assistance** – Eclipse has key bindings that has more than one key stroke. Examples of such key bindings are Ctrl+X S (Save in the Emacs key configuration) or Alt+Shift+Q Y (Show View (View: Synchronize) in the default key configuration). It is hard to learn these keys, and it can also be hard to remember them if you don't use them often. If you initiate such a key sequence and wait a second, a little pop-up showing you the possible completions will appear.
- **Customizing toolbar and menu bar** – *Window dropdown menu* → *Perspective* → *Customize Perspective.* The screen has 4 tabs, Toolbar visibility, Menu Visibility Action Set Visibility and Shortcuts.
- **Restoring deleted resources** – You can select container resource and use Restore from Local History to restore deleted files. You can restore more than one file at one time.

Workbench Tips and Tricks - continued

Restoring deleted resources from local histo₁

To restore a deleted Workbench resource with a state from the local history:

1. In one of the navigation views, select the folder or project into which you want to restore history state.
2. From the resource's pop-up menu, select **Restore from Local History**.... The Restore F₁ History dialog opens showing all files that were previously contained in the selected folk and all of their sub-folders.
3. Check the files that you want to restore
4. If you don't want to restore just the last state of a file you can select any other state of the the **Local History** list on the right hand side of the dialog. The bottom pane of the dialog contents of the state.
5. If you are done with all files click **Restore**.

Tip: You can configure your Workbench preferences to specify how many days to keep files, c entries per file you want to keep, or the maximum file size for files to be kept with the ⊕ **Gen** **Workspace > Local History** preference page.

- **Quickly find a resource** - From *the Navigate download menu* → *Goto* → *what resource* you are looking for.

- **Copying and moving resources** - You can drag and drop files and folders within the Project Explorer view to move them around. Hold down the **Ctrl** key to make copies.

- **Exporting files –** The Export XML Caché Script wizard allows you to export Atelier source files in a number of different ways.

- **Import files –** You can quickly import files and folders into your workspace by dragging them from the file system (e.g., from a Windows Explorer window) and dropping them into the Project Explorer view. The files and folder are always copied into the project; the originals are not affected.

- **Transfer preferences** - The preferences can be transferred from one workspace to another by exporting and importing them. In addition, it is possible to only do this for selected categories . . . .

- **Workspace project management** - Use the *Project download menu >* *Close Project command* menu to manage projects within your workspace. When a project is closed, its resources are temporarily "offline" and no longer appear in the Workbench.

— Workbench Tips and Tricks - continued

- **Describing your configuration** - When reporting a problem, it is often important to capture details about your setup. The Installation Details button on the command link *Help download menu → About Product* menu opens a dialog containing pages that describe different aspects of the installation. The Configuration page displays a file containing various pieces of information about the setup.
- **Filtering resources** - Most views that show resources support filtering of the items. You control which items are visible by applying filters or working sets. The commands to filter are found in the view menu.
- **Quick fix in Tasks view** - You can use the Quick Fix command in the Tasks view to suggest an automatic fix for the selected item.
- **Creating path variables** - When creating a linked folder or file, you can specify the target location relative to a path variable.
- **Comparing zip archives with each other or with a folder**
  Select two zip archives or one archive and a folder in the resource Project Explorer view and choose *Compare With → Each Other* from the view's popup menu.
- **Switch workspace** - Instead of shutting down eclipse and restarting with a different workspace you can instead use *File dropdown menu → Switch Workspace.*
- **Show workspace path** use the *Windows dropdown menu → Preference General → Workspace path.*
- **Always run in background** - use the *Windows dropdown menu → Preference General → Always run in background.*
- **Launch multiple configurations sequentially** – You can create a *Launch Group* via the *Run dropdown menu → Run Configurations...* or *Run dropdown menu → Debug Configurations...* dialog to launch multiple launch configurations sequentially, with configurable actions after launching each group member.
- **Sort breakpoints by creation time** - You can use the *Breakpoint dropdown menu Sort By → Creation Time* option to show the newly created breakpoints on top.

Editing Tips and Tricks

Here is a subject listing of the Editing Tips and Tricks. You will need to go into Eclipse/Atelier to see exactly how they work.

- **Finding a string incrementally**

  Use *Edit* → *Incremental Find Next* (Ctrl+J) or

  Edit → *Incremental Find Previous* (Ctrl+Shift+J)

  Enter the incremental find mode and start typing the string to match, matches are found incrementally as you type.

  The search string is shown in the status line.

  Press Ctrl+J to go to the next match.

  Press Ctrl+Shift+J to go to the previous match.

  Press Enter or Esc to exit incremental find mode.

- **Go to last edit location**

  Navigate → *Go to Last Edit Location* (Ctrl+Q) takes you back to the place where you last made a change. A corresponding button marked *Go to last edit position icon* is shown in the toolbar. If this toolbar button does not appear in your perspective, you can add it by selecting command link *Window dropdown menu* → *Perspective* → *Customize Perspective*, then *Other* → *Editor Navigation*.

- **Shortcuts for manipulating lines**

  All text editors based on the Eclipse editor framework support editing functions, including

  - Moving lines up Alt+Arrow Up
  - Moving lines down Alt+Arrow Down
  - Copying lines up Ctrl+Alt+Arrow Up
  - Copying lines down Ctrl+Alt+Arrow Down
  - Inserting a new line above Ctrl+Shift+Enter
  - Inserting a new line below Shift+Enter
  - Converting to lowercase Ctrl+Shift+Y
  - Converting to uppercase Ctrl+Shift+X.

Editing Tips and Tricks – continued

- **Quick Diff: seeing what has changed as you edit**

  Quick Diff provides color-coded change indication while you are typing. It can be turned on for text editors using either the ruler context menu, Ctrl+Shift+Q or for all new editors on the *Windows dropdown menu* → *Perference* → *General* → *Editors* → *Text Editors* → *Quick Diff*. The colors show additions, deletions, and changes to the editor buffer as compared to a reference, for example, the contents of the file on disk or its latest CVS revision.

- **Customizing the presentation of annotations**

  You can customize the presentation of annotations in editors on the *Windows dropdown menu* → *Preference* → *General* → *Editors* → *Text Editors* → *Annotations*.

- **Next / previous navigation**

  You can use Ctrl+. to navigate to the next search match, editor error, or compare difference.

  You can use Ctrl+, to navigate to the previous search match, editor error, or compare difference.

  These are the shortcut keys for *Navigate > Next and Navigate > Previous*.

- **Word completion**

  In any text editor you can complete a prefix to a word occurring in all currently open editors or buffers. The default key binding for word completion is Alt+/ (*Ctrl+. on the Mac*).

- **Open untitled files**

  A text editor can be opened without creating a file first: select *File dropdown menu* → *New* → *Untitled Text File*.

- **Commands to zoom in text editors**

  In text editors, you can use

  Zoom In Ctrl++ or Ctrl+= and

  Zoom Out Ctrl+-

  commands to increase and decrease the font size.

Help Tips and Tricks Buttons

Here is a listing of some the Help Tips and Tricks Buttons.

- **Show in external window**

    Having trouble reading help topics from the Help view/tray? Use the Show in external window button from the toolbar to view the document in the full help window.

- **Find that topic**

    While browsing a searched topic, you can find out where that *topic is in the table of contents* by using the *Show in table of contents* button in the toolbar.

- **Bookmarks**

    You can keep your own list of bookmarks to pages in help books. Create a bookmark with the Bookmark document icon button on the toolbar of the Help browser. The bookmarks show up in the Bookmarks icon Bookmarks tab.

Help Tips and Tricks – continued

- **Infopops**

  If you prefer the yellow pop-ups (infopops) used in previous releases for context-sensitive help, you can configure Help to use these instead of *Windows dropdown menu* → *Preference* → *Help*.

- **Cheat Sheets**

  Cheat sheets provide step by step guidance on how to perform common tasks. To see what cheat sheets exist use the command link *Help* → *dropdown menu* → *Cheat Sheets... menu item*. This menu item may not appear in all perspectives.

- **Cheat Sheet State**

  A cheat sheet will remember which steps you have performed even if you close the cheat sheet view, open another cheat sheet or exit Eclipse

Chapter 9 - Object Basics

Goals of Object Technology

One of the primary goals of Object Technology is that the data and the code that changes the data should reside together.

In legacy data processing there was the data sitting in one set of files and then the code or executables residing somewhere else.

When updates to the data were to occur, the data would be brought out and the executables would be applied to the data, thus updating the data. There are several problems with this process, one of the primary is that code that updated the data would be in a number of different places and this yielded redundant code.

It becomes difficult to change the code because the code for one particular data item could exist in a number of different places.

With Object Technology the data and the code that modifies the data exist in the same place, in the Class. Code that updates the data exist in one and only one place, with rare and well documented exceptions. This eliminates redundant code. When the code needs to be changed, there is one and only one place to look, in the Class.

Let me state though that the Object approach does not solve all data processing problems, it does however help in this area of redundant code.

Terms of Object Technology

Please note – these terms are simplified for easy understanding, and as such are subject to interpretation and possible correction depending on who is doing the defining. They can and often do become much more complicated.

Class

Class is the basic building block of Object Technology. Among other items a Class contains *data* and *methods*. Once a Class is instantiated, it is said to have become an Object.

Object Technology is based upon the concept of a *Class*. This Class contains Data and Methods. The Methods inside the Class is the only acceptable means of changing the Data inside the Class. This is one of the most important principles of Object Technology, that is the Data and the Methods are together inside the Class.

Once an instance of a Class is instantiated, it thus becomes one *Object* of the Class.

In legacy programming the data and the methods were separated. This cause redundancy in methods, there may have been multiple methods that change the data.

Data

Data (within a Class) – this is the data of the Object itself. This data is normally broken down into *Fields*.

Methods

Methods are executable code, this code modifies the data that co-exist with it in a Class. This is one of the tenants of Object Technology, data and methods co-exist inside a Class and the methods are the only place that changes the data. Hence this eliminates code redundancy and with the code in the class there is no hunting for the relevant code when changes are necessary.

Class Methods

Class Method is just a type of Method. Class Methods may be called without an instantiated Object as opposed to Instance Methods which needs an instantiated Object to be called. A Method must be either a Class Method or an Instance Method.

Instance Methods

Instance Methods is just a type of Method. An Instance Method must be called by an instantiated Object as opposed to a Class Method which may be called without an instantiated Object. A Method must be either a Class Method or an Instance Method.

Instantiation

The process where a Class (or other item) comes alive or becomes an active part of memory. Once a Class is instantiated, it becomes an Object.

Inheritance

Inheritance is the process by which one Class inherits data, methods, or attributes from another class.

Encapsulation

Encapsulation has to do with security, that a class encapsulates or hides it data and methods so others cannot view them.

Oref

Object Reference. An Oref is a variable that contains all information of a Class instance in-memory.

Polymorphism

Poly – many, morphism – change. This allows Classes to inherit a Method or other items from another Class, changing it for its own purposes.

There are many more terms and the terms already given may have further sub-divisions. But hopefully this will give you some idea of Object Technology as you learn more.

Invoking a Class Method

The following concepts are introduced here and will be expanded upon and hopefully will become clearer in chapters to come.

In native Caché and MUMPS, the traditional way to invoke an executable procedure is with a DO, or DO While or sometimes with a $, or $$, or Call or even $$$ for a Macro.

In Object Technology the syntax to execute a Class Method within a Class is:

Set Oref=##class(Package.ClassName).%Method(Param)

Where:

- **Oref** – an Oref represents an Object Reference. What this means is that this is the result from calling an Executable Procedure of a Class. The output from calling this class is placed in the variable "Oref". Another way to think of an Oref is that it is an "in-memory" representation of the Class. This class typically contains data and executable procedures.

- **##class** – Object Technology "call" which invokes this method within this class

- **Package** – package or schema part of the class name

- **ClassName** – just that, the name of the class

- **%Method** – "Class Method" within the class

- **Param** – any parameters being passed

Invoking a Method

To invoke a Method, as opposed to a Class Method, that class needs to be already instantiated, or already "in-memory."

Set Oref=##class(Package.ClassName).%New()

> To create a new empty Oref of the Class based on the %New executable. For a definition of Oref see the previous page.

Now that we have a new empty Oref (Object Reference) of the Class, we can make calls into the Class.

Do Oref.Method(param)

> Here we call the Method of the Oref Class passing it whatever parameters are necessary.

Or

Write Oref.Method(param) – if the method returns a value

Set X=Oref.Method(param) – if the method returns a value

> Here we call the Method and accept whatever value the Method passes back.

Other Object Methods

Here are some other examples of calling Object Method.

Opening a new Object

>   Set Oref=##class(Package.ClassName).%New()

Opening an existing Object when the Id is already known.

>   Set Oref=##class(Package.ClassName).%OpenId(Id)

Seeing if an ID Exists

>   Write ##class(Sample.Person).%ExistsId(1)

Seeing if a Variables is a valid Object

>   If $IsObject(Oref)

Display an Error

>   This call is used when "Status" is an error.

>   If Status '= 1 Write $SYSTEM.OBJ.DisplayError(Status)

A word to the wise ain't necessary –

it's the stupid ones that need the advice

Bill Cosby

Chapter 10 - Studio Routine

This chapter is for working in Studio, the chapters for working in Studio are 10, 12, 14, and 16.

SLastNameRoutine

In this chapter we will create a Routine in Studio.

The Routine name we will use is *SLastNameRoutine.*

> The S is for Studio,
>
> LastName is for your last name, and
>
> Routine of course is "Routine."

My last name is Kadow, so the Class name I would use is *SKADOWROUTINE.*

This is to avoid confusion later and to identify your classes in case others on your system are going through the same book.

Creating a Routine in Studio

Here we are going to create a Caché Routine using Studio.

Start Caché Studio from the Caché Cube, the Caché Cube is the small bluish cube in the system tray.

If you have not used Caché Studio before you will need to see Chapter 4 on Caché Software Installation.

Startup Caché Studio

Click on the small blueish cube in your system tray.

The following menu will appear, click on "Studio".

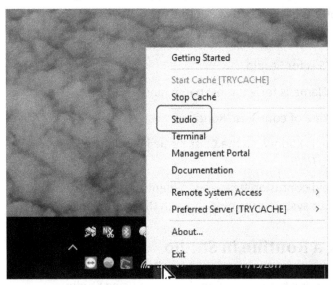

Once inside Caché Studio, (you may need to enter a username and password).

Now click on the File Menu (upper left) and Change the Namespace to "User". You can also hit F4 to change your namespace.

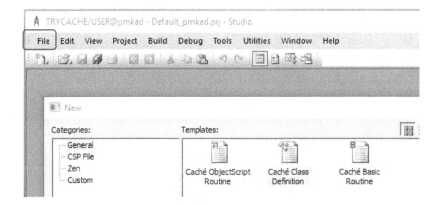

If your configuration does not have a Namespace of "User", I suggest you use whatever namespace you normally test with. You may need to get permission from your manager or project leader.

One word of clarification, here a Routine is called "ObjectScript Routine". The word "ObjectScript" may be confusing. We are not creating Objects here, "ObjectScript" is referring to the programming language used in creating a Routine, not referring to "Objects."

From the File Menu select *New*. A selection box will come up, ensure the Category is on General, and select Caché ObjectScript Routine Definition.

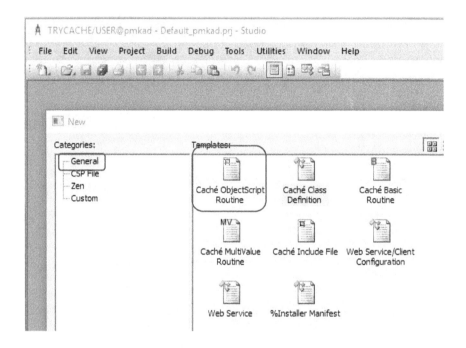

A blank screen will come up like the one below.

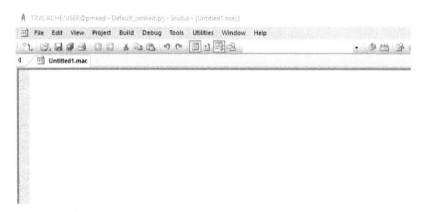

Routine Name

From the File dropdown menu in the upper left-hand corner click on SaveAs.

Now enter the Routine name of SLastNameRoutine. Ensure that the "Look in:" has a value of "USER".

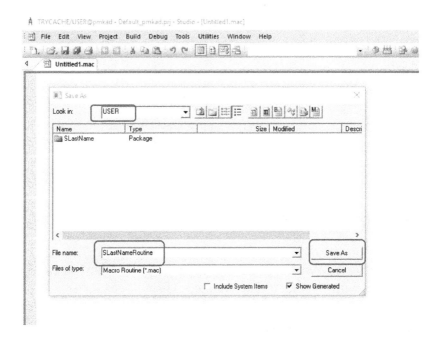

Then Click on SaveAs.

Enter Code in Routine

Enter the code below in your Routine.

```
SLastNameRoutine

    Set Counter=0
Loop
    Set Counter=Counter+1
    Write !,"Counter: ",Counter
    If Counter>5 Quit
    Goto Loop
```

Then under the Build dropdown menu select Compile or type Ctrl-F7 .

To run your code you need to bring up the Terminal from the Caché Cube and type Do ^SLastNameRoutine.

Run Studio Routine

```
USER>d ^SLastNameRoutine

Counter: 1
Counter: 2
Counter: 3
Counter: 4
Counter: 5
Counter: 6
USER>
```

Debug Studio Routine

Using the Debug dropdown menu, you can run your code and debug it at the same time.

From the Debug Target option give your code a starting point, like Loop.

Then use the Breakpoint option to specify the various breakpoints you want. You can also use the F9 key to set a breakpoint when the cursor is sitting on the line. F9 will only work if the routine is freshly compiled.

Then use the Go to start the routine and Step into, Step Over, and Step out to control execution.

Hover over variables to see their value, or Write them in the Output screen.

You can see the other options under the Debug dropdown menu. The options also have keyboard shortcuts.

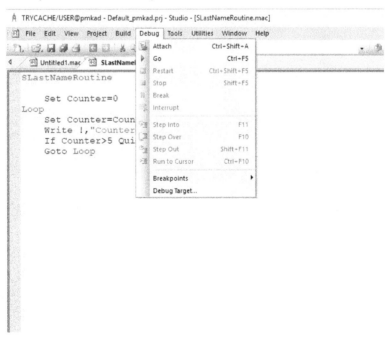

The message below is a lie,
The message above is the truth..

Chapter 11 - Atelier Routine

> This chapter is for working in Atelier, the chapters for working in Atelier are 11, 13, 15, and 17.

ALastNameRoutine

In this chapter we will create a Routine in Atelier.

The Routine name we will use is *ALastNameRoutine.*

>   The A is for Atelier,
>
>   LastName is for your last name, and
>
>   Routine of course is "Routine."

My last name is Kadow, so the Class name I would use is *AKADOWROUTINE.*

This is to avoid confusion later and to identify your classes in case others on your system are going through the same book.

Creating a Routine in Atelier

Here we are going to create a Caché Routine using Atelier.

Start Caché Studio from the Caché Cube, the Caché Cube is the small bluish cube in the system tray.
We will now step through creating a Routine in Atelier like we did in Caché Studio.

Startup Eclipse

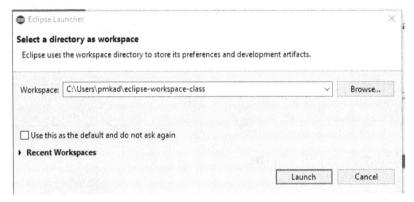

Click on the Workbench.

Atelier Class Cheat Sheet

You may also create an Atelier Routine using a Cheat Sheet.

Go to Help → Cheat Sheet → Atelier → Create an Atelier Routine

Set your Perspective to Atelier

Now set your Perspective to Atelier.

This is assuming you have already loaded the Atelier Plug-in, see Atelier Plug-in into Eclipse in Chapter 4.

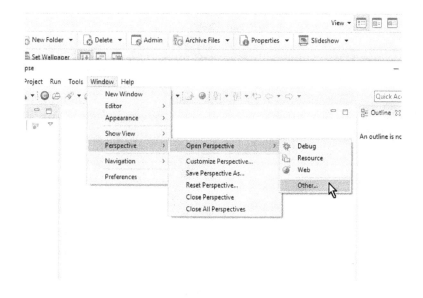

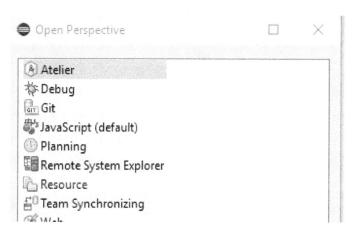

Create a new project

From the Workbench, click on the File dropdown menu (upper left), then New and then Atelier project.

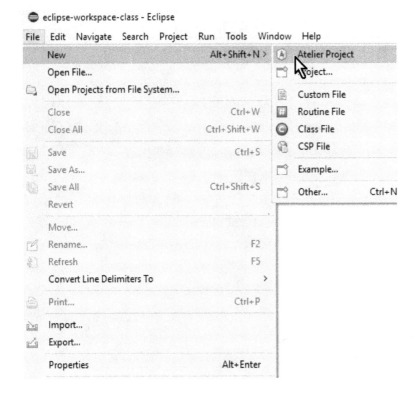

Select and/or Create Project

Enter TeamA for Project. This project can be whatever you or your manager wants. But now we will use "TeamA".

Enter the Connection Configuration, see topic *Configuring a Server Connection* in Chapter 5 if you need to.

Then enter Namespace.

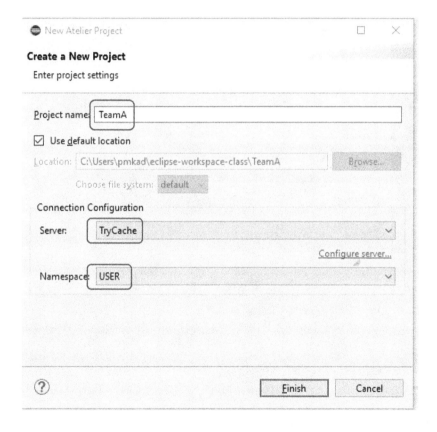

Select Routine File

Next click on the File Menu (upper left), then New and then Routine File.

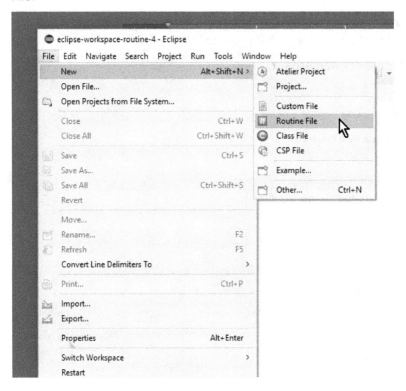

Select COS Routine

Select COS Routine, COS stands for Caché ObjectScript.

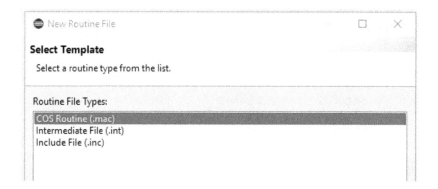

Enter COS Routine Information

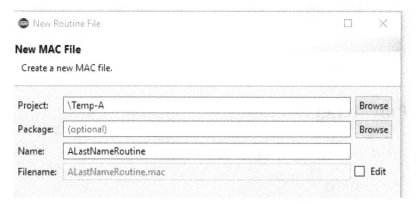

Enter the Project and Routine name, ALastNameRoutine.

Enter Routine Code

Add the following code in your Routine.

ALastNameRoutine.mac ⊠

```
1  ROUTINE ALastNameRoutine
2    Set Counter=0
3  Loop
4    Set Counter=Counter+1
5    If Counter>5 Quit
6    Write !,"Counter: ",Counter
7    Goto Loop
8
```

After entering the code, select the File dropdown menu and select save.

To run your code you need to bring up the Terminal from the Caché Cube and type Do ^ALastNameRoutine.

Run Atelier Routine

```
USER>Do ^ALastNameRoutine

Counter: 1
Counter: 2
Counter: 3
Counter: 4
Counter: 5
USER>
```

Another way to Run your code, click on the Run dropdown Menu.

It may ask for what application to run under, select Atelier.

```
ALastNameRoutine.mac
1  ROUTINE ALastNameRoutine
2    Set Counter=0
3  Loop
4    Set Counter=Counter+1
5    If Counter>5 Quit
6    Write !,"Counter: ",Counter
7    Goto Loop
8
```

Console   Tasks   Problems   Atelier Documentation

<terminated> [Debug Console] ALastNameRoutine [Atelier Application]

```
Counter: 1
Counter: 2
Counter: 3
Counter: 4
Counter: 5
```

Debug Atelier Routine

To debug your code, select the debug dropdown menu. It will ask if you wish to switch to the debug perspective.

You can set breakpoints by double clicking on the blue area in the margin.

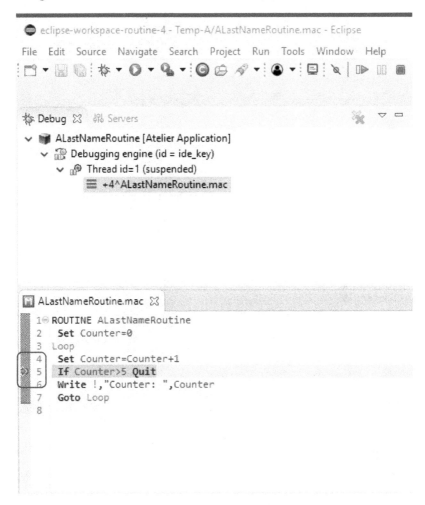

Debug Control

Under the run dropdown menu, you can see the debug control options; Step Into, Step Over, Step Return, etc.

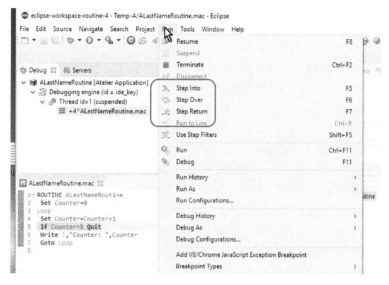

A lot of people are afraid of heights.

Not me, I'm afraid of widths

Steven Wright.

Chapter 12 - Studio Class

This chapter is for working in Studio, the chapters for working in Studio are 10, 12, 14, and 16.

SLastName.Person

In this chapter we will create an Object Class in Studio.

The Class name we will use is *SLastName.Person.*

> The S is for Studio,
>
> LastName is for your last name, and
>
> Person is for "Person".

My last name is Kadow, so the Class name I would use is *SKADOW.PERSON.*

This is to avoid confusion later and to identify your classes in case others on your system are going through the same book.

Creating a Class in Studio

Here we are going to create a Caché Class using Studio.

Start Caché Studio from the Caché Cube, the Caché Cube is the small bluish cube in the system tray.

If you have not used Caché Studio before you will need to see Chapter 4 on Caché Software Installation.

The Class – Basic Structure

The *Object Class* is the basic structure in Object Technology. It is a template for holding Data and Methods. These Methods in this class are for the sole purpose of changing the Data in this class.

Having Data and Methods together is one of the most important principles in Object Technology.

Once we have defined our Data, then we will create our Methods.

Creating a Class in Studio

Here we are going to create a Caché Class using Studio.

Start Caché Studio from the Caché Cube, the Caché Cube is the small bluish cube in the system tray.

If you have not used Caché Studio before you will need to see Chapter 4 on Caché Software Installation.

Startup Caché Studio

Click on the small blueish cube in your system tray.

The following menu will appear, click on "Studio".

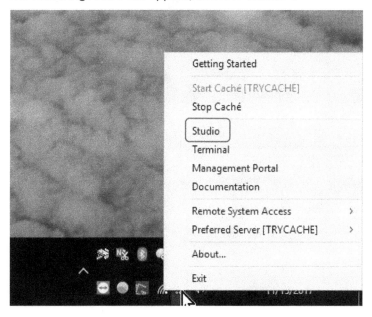

Once inside Caché Studio, (you may need to enter a username and password) click on the File Menu (upper left) and Change the Namespace to "User". You can also hit F4 to change your namespace.

If your configuration does not have a Namespace of "User", I suggest you use whatever namespace you normally test with. You may need to get permission from your manager or project leader.

From the File Menu select *New*. A selection box will come up, ensure the Category is on General, and select Caché Class Definition.

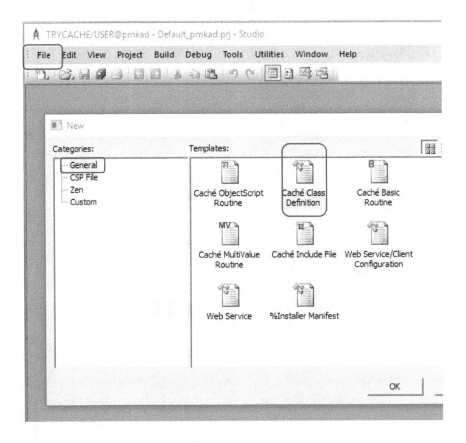

See the heading under SLastName.Person several pages up to insert the Package and Class name.

Class Name

There are two pieces to a Class name, separated by a period. The piece before the period is called the Package or Schema and piece two after the period is called the Name.

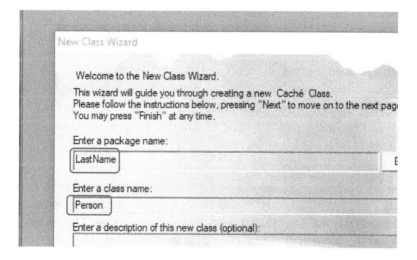

Click on the Next button. For Class Type (next screen) take the defaults. On the following screen select XML Enabled and Data Population, then hit Finish.

Create the SLastName.Person Class

Your class should look like the one below.

```
/// Person Class for Studio
Class SLastName.Person Extends (%Persistent, %Populate, %XML.Adaptor)
{

}
```

Go to the Build dropdown menu and choose the compile option. You can also compile your class by typing Ctrl+F7. In addition to compiling your class it is a good idea to save your class. Look for the asterisk next to the class name, if an asterisk is there, the class is not compiled.

Notice the word "Extends" in the above example. It means that the Class extends the %Persistent class, or is based on that Class as well as the %Populate and %XML.Adaptor class. This is part of Inheritance, that this class inherits properties and methods from these other classes.

Add a Name Property and Index to your Class

In this section, we will be adding a Name Property and Index.

Copy into your class the lines shown below.

```
/// Person Class for Studio
Class SLastName.Person Extends (%Persistent, %Populate, %XM]
{

Property Name As %Name(POPSPEC = "Name()") [ Required ];

Index NameIndex On Name;
```

For the Name property, we used a data type of %Name, %Name has a built–in format of "Last, First", but don't be concerned about that now.

We will explain what the *POPSPEC* parameter does later.

Compile your class and pay attention to any compile error message.

Class, Routine, SQL Table

Take note of the Output box in Studio, not only a Class is created, but a Routine and a SQL Table is created as well, this is the default behavior for Caché.

For all Classes, Caché creates three elements or files:

1. a Class,
2. a Routine, and
3. a SQL Table.

Caché ensures these three will always be in sync.

Default Storage

When you compile your class, you will notice a Default Storage section added to your class. That is how Caché allocates its storage. But for the time being you can safely ignore that part.

Adding Data to SLastName.Person

Type the follow script in the Caché *Terminal* to add actual data to your class. This will create three objects based on your class.

```
USER>

USER>Zn "User"    ;change namespace to user

USER>Set Oref=##class(SLastName.Person).%New()

USER>Set Oref.Name="Dover, Ben"

USER>Write Oref.%Save()
1
USER>Set Oref=##class(SLastName.Person).%New()

USER>Set Oref.Name="Dover, Ilene"

USER>Write Oref.%Save()
1
USER>Set Oref=##class(SLastName.Person).%New()

USER>Set Oref.Name="Dover, Fred"

USER>Write Oref.%Save()
1
USER>D ^%G

For help on global specifications DO HELP^%G
Global ^SLastName.PersonD
^SLastName.PersonD
3
^SLastName.PersonD(1)=$lb("","Dover, Ben")
               2)=$lb("","Dover, Ilene")
               3)=$lb("","Dover, Fred")
```

The script on the previous page was done in Caché Terminal and shows how to add Data to your class.

Set Oref=##class(SLastName.Person).%New()

This line creates a new empty instance of our class in-memory.

Set Oref.Name="Dover, Ben"

This line adds the name Ben Dover to the Name variable in the in-memory class.

Write Oref.%Save()

This line saves the instance, the "1" show the add was successful.

^SLastName.PersonD=3

^SLastName.PersonD(1)=$lb("","Dover, Ben")

^SLastName.PersonD(2)=$lb("","Dover, Ilene")

^SLastName.PersonD(3)=$lb("","Dover, Fred")

Here we see that the data was added to our Class, which is actually the Global ^SLastName.PersonD

Difference between a Class and an Object

In this example, we added 3 people to the Class; Ben Dover, Ilene Dover and Fred Dover. We created three new objects (one for each person) based on the SLastName.Person class.

Here is the difference between a Class and an Object. A class is just a template or pattern. Whereas an Object is a populated class normally in-memory. In a sense when an instance for a class has data and is in-memory it "comes alive", or is *instantiated*.

Saving your Class

Ensure when you Write the Oref.%Save command, a 1 is returned, otherwise your data was not saved. The %Save method is a member of the %Persistent class. Your class inherited this method from the %Persistent class when you included %Persistent in the Extends statement.

He's so snobbish he has an unlisted zip-code

Earl Wilson.

Chapter 13 - Atelier Class

This chapter is for working in Atelier, the chapters for working in Atelier are 11, 13, 15, and 17.

ALastName.Person

In this chapter we will create an Object Class in Atelier.

The Class name we will use is *ALastName.Person*.

>The A is for Atelier,
>
>LastName is for your last name, and
>
>Person is for "Person".

My last name is Kadow, so the Class name I would use is *AKADOW.PERSON*.

This is to avoid confusion later and to identify your classes in case others on your system are going through the same book.

The Class – Basic Structure

The *Object Class* is the basic structure in Object Technology. It is a template for holding Data and Methods. These Methods in this class are for the sole purpose of changing the Data in this class.

Having Data and Methods together is one of the most important principles in Object Technology.

Once we have defined our Data, then we will create our Methods.

Creating a Class in Atelier

Please note the documentation has extensive information on how to create a new empty class in Atelier. but this chapter is not using it. However, feel free to use it as a reference point.

InterSystems Atelier User Guide → Reference → New Class File

InterSystems Atelier User Guide > Reference > New Class File

New Empty Class

This page contains the following fields you can use to provide information about the new class:

Option	Description	Default
Project	The project that contains the new file. Use the **Browse** button to select a project. The **Browse** button opens a dialog that lists projects in the workspace. The text field at the top of the dialog lets you enter filter text to limit the list of projects. The new file is created in the folder associated with the project, which is commonly a folder in the workspace with the same name as the project. In cases where the project was not created in the default location, the folder can have a different name and location. The **Properties** view shows the actual location in the file system for projects and files.	The currently selected project.
Package	The name of the Caché package associated with this file. Use the **Browse** button to search for a package.	User
Name	The name of the class	
Filename	The name of the new file.	A file name composed of the package name, and the class name in the format **package.class**.
Edit	If selected, allows you to specify a filename other than the default	Unselected

Atelier Class Cheat Sheet

You may also create an Atelier Class using a Cheat Sheet.

Go to Help → Cheat Sheet → Atelier → Create an Atelier Class

The Class in Atelier

All Atelier Class files will have an extension of ".cls".

We will now step through creating a Class in Atelier like we did in Caché Studio.

Startup Eclipse.

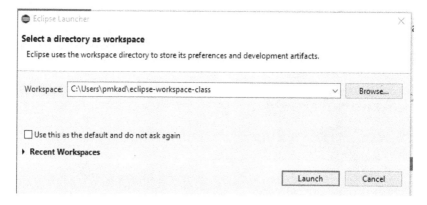

Click on the Workbench.

Set your Perspective to Atelier

This is assuming you already loaded the Atelier Plug-in, see Atelier Plug-in into Eclipse in Chapter 4.

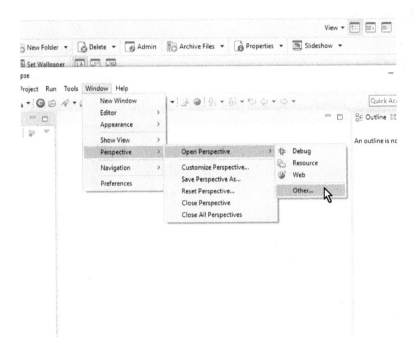

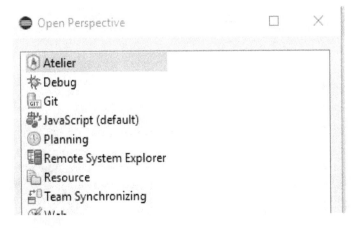

Set your Perspective to Atelier

Once inside the Workbench, click on the File dropdown menu (upper left), then New and then Atelier project.

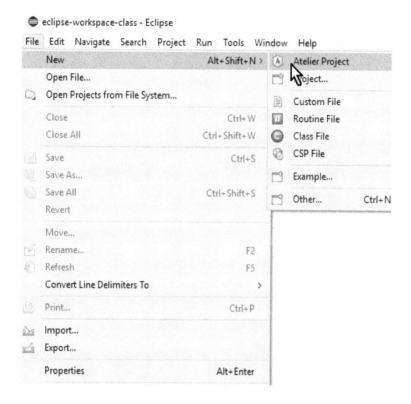

Select and/or Create Project

Enter TeamA for Project. This project can be whatever you or your manager wants. But now we will use "TeamA".

Enter the Connection Configuration, see topic *Configuring a Server Connection* in Chapter 5 and the enter Namespace.

Select Class File

Next click on the File Menu (upper left), then New and then Class File.

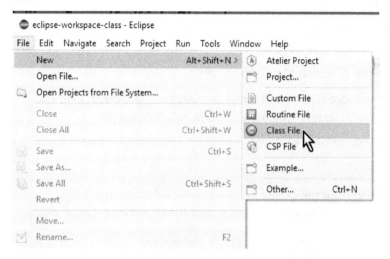

Template Page

Click Next to bypass the Template page or enter a Template if you have one.

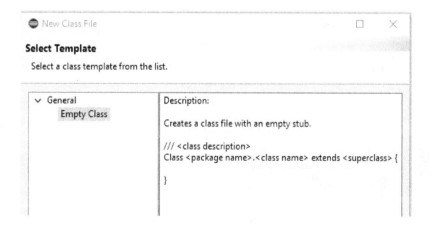

New Empty Class File

Enter information for the Class you are going to create

TeamA for Project.

See the heading under ALastName.Person several pages up to insert the Package and Class name.

Click the %Persistent button.

Hit the More button and scroll through the available classes and find the %Library.Populate Class and %XML.Adapter.

The description is optional.

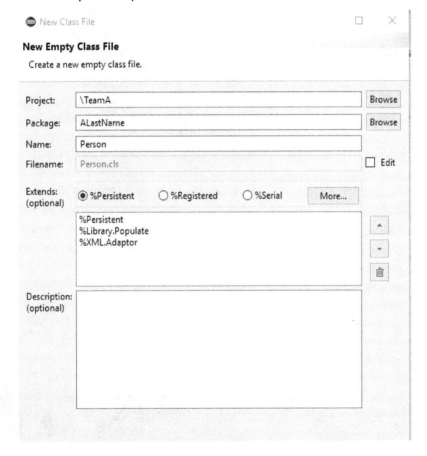

Your class should look something like the following.

```
ALastName/Person.cls - Eclipse
:h  Project  Run  Tools  Window  Help

Person.cls

1  Class ALastName.Person Extends (%Persistent,%Library.Populate,%XML.Adaptor)
2  {
3
4  }
```

Add Two Lines

Add the following two lines to your class.

```
TeamA/ALastName/Person.cls - Eclipse
:  Search  Project  Run  Tools  Window  Help

*Person.cls

1  Class ALastName.Person Extends (%Persistent,%Library.Populat
2  {
3
4  Property Name As %Name(POPSPEC = "Name()") [Required ];
5
6  Index NameIndex On Name;
7
8  }
```

This is one area where Atelier differs from Studio.

Content Assist.

We will use something call *Content Assist.*

Position your cursor between the { and }

Go to the Edit dropdown menu and click on Content Assist.

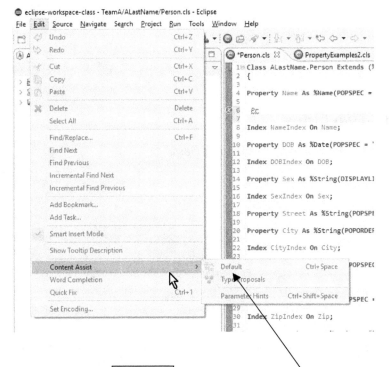

Then either type Ctrl+Space or click on the Default button. It may take a few tries to get it correct. But you should be able to select which parameter you want.

Content Assist gives you a template of what you need. From the *As Type* to the *///documentation* on the line before.

It provides you with a number of templates, for example:

➢ Class

➢ ClassMethod

➢ Do While

➢ For

➢ For List

➢ For Loop

➢ If Construct

➢ If Else If Else

➢ Property

➢ Parameter

Content Assist can be used in a number of different ways. See Appendix H.

Save ALastName.Person

Lastly click File and then Save.

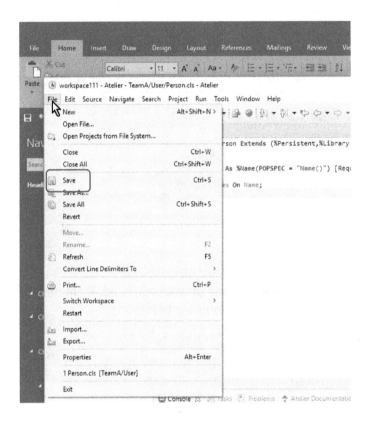

Adding Data to ALastName.Person

Type the follow script in the Caché *Terminal* to add actual data to your class. This will create three objects based on your class.

```
USER>Zn "User"    ;change namespace to user

USER>Set Oref=##class(ALastName.Person).%New()

USER>Set Oref.Name="Dover, Ben"

USER>Write Oref.%Save() ;
1
USER>Set Oref=##class(ALastName.Person).%New()

USER>Set Oref.Name="Dover, Ilene"

USER>Write Oref.%Save() ;
1
USER>Set Oref=##class(ALastName.Person).%New()

USER>Set Oref.Name="Dover, Fred"

USER>Write Oref.%Save() ;
1
USER>D ^%G

Device:
Right margin: 80 =>
Screen size for paging (0=nopaging)? 24 =>
For help on global specifications DO HELP^%G
Global ^ALastName.PersonD
^ALastName.PersonD
3
^ALastName.PersonD(1)=$lb("","Dover, Ben")
             2)=$lb("","Dover, Ilene")
             3)=$lb("","Dover, Fred")
```

The script on the previous page was done in Caché Terminal and shows how to add Data to your class.

Set Oref=##class(ALastName.Person).%New()

This line creates a new empty instance of our class in-memory.

Set Oref.Name="Dover, Ben"

This line adds the name Ben Dover to the Name variable in the in-memory class.

Write Oref.%Save()

This line saves the instance, the "1" show the add was successful

^ALastName.PersonD=3

^ALastName.PersonD(1)=$lb("","Dover, Ben")

^ALastName.PersonD(2)=$lb("","Dover, Ilene")

^ALastName.PersonD(3)=$lb("","Dover, Fred")

Here we see that the data was added to our Class, which is actually the Global ^ALastName.PersonD

Difference between a Class and an Object

In this example, we added 3 people to the Class; Ben Dover, Ilene Dover and Fred Dover. We created three new objects (one for each person) based on the ALastName.Person class.

Here is the difference between a Class and an Object. A class is just a template or pattern. Whereas an Object is a populated class normally in-memory. In a sense when an instance for a class has data and is in-memory it "comes alive", or is *instantiated*.

Saving your Class

Ensure when you Write the Oref.%Save command, a 1 is returned, otherwise your data was not saved. The %Save method is a member of the %Persistent class. Your class inherited this method from the %Persistent class when you included %Persistent in the Extends statement.

The biggest argument against democracy is a five minute discussion with the average vote

Winston Churchill.

Chapter 14 - Studio Properties

This chapter is for working in Studio, the chapters for working in Studio are 10, 12, 14, and 16.

SLastName.Person

In this chapter we will modify an Object Class in Studio.

The Class name we will use is *SLastName.Person.*

> The S is for Studio,
>
> LastName is for your last name, and
>
> Person is for "Person".

My last name is Kadow, so the Class name I would use is *SKADOW.PERSON.*

This is to avoid confusion later and to identify your classes in case others on your system are going through the same book.

Adding more Properties to the SLastName.Person Class

Now we are going to add a few more properties to the SLastName.Person Class.

Here is a list of the properties we are adding:

- DOB and DOBIndex, (date of birth)
- Sex, (M/F)
- Street address
- City and CityIndex,
- State and StateIndex,

- Zip and ZipIndex.

Add the new lines on the next page.

Property Wizard

You may either retype the lines as I have them on the next page or try your hand at adding them through the *Property Wizard*. To use the Property Wizard, click on the Class menu, select Add, and then select Property.

I would recompile after every line to ensure you have a clean compile.

There are other helpful Wizards inside Studio. I would get into the habit of using the dropdown menus at the top of Studio until you are more familiar with the format of the commands.

```
◁   SLastName.Person.cls
 SLastName.Person.cls
     /// Person Class for Studio
     Class SLastName.Person Extends (%Persistent, %Populate, %XML.Adaptor)
     {

     Property Name As %Name(POPSPEC = "Name()") [ Required ];

     Index NameIndex On Name;

     Property DOB As %Date(POPSPEC = "Date()") [ Required ];

     Index DOBIndex On DOB;

     Property Sex As %String(DISPLAYLIST = ",Male,Female", VALUELIST = ",M,F") [ Required ];

     Index SexIndex On Sex;

     Property Street As %String(POPSPEC = "Street()") [ Required ];

     Property City As %String(POPORDER = "City()") [ Required ];

     Index CityIndex On City;

     Property State As %String(POPSPEC = "USState()") [ Required ];

     Index StateIndex On State;

     Property Zip As %String(POPSPEC = "USZip()") [ Required ];

     Index ZipIndex On Zip;
```

Data Population

InterSystems built into Caché some utility applications. One of these is the *Populate Utility*. It is one of their better ideas.

Data population is where dummy data or test data fills up your database, as much as you specify.

Many of the data types have this capability, like name, date, street, city, ssn, etc. And even those data types that do not have this capability, you can build it in yourself with a little extra coding.

Look at your class and all the properties that have the POPSPEC parameter. We are now going to use the POPSPEC parameter to add dummy data to your database.

Populate Documentation

From the Caché Cube in the system tray, select Documentation. Then Search for *Populate*.

Or use the link *http://doc.intersystems.com/* , select the version of documentation you want, and search from there.

Populate the Class

Now that you have included %Populate in the Class Extends statement and set up the POPSPEC parameters, all you have to do is issue the following command in the Caché Terminal

Cache TRM:8928 (TRYCACHE)

File   Edit   Help

```
Node: PMKADOW, Instance: TRYCACHE

Username: pmkad
Password: ***
USER>

USER>Write ##class(SLastName.Person).Populate(100)
100
USER>
```

So, with one command, we can create 100 or more instances or objects of your class, very cool!

Now you can run SQL and see all the data it returns.

Using SQL to see your data

From the Caché Cube in your system tray, select *Terminal*.

Type in the commands from the following example.

As you can see IDs 1,2,3 are for Ben, Ilene and Fred Dover we added initially. For the rest of the IDs through 100 all have full data.

```
USER>DO $SYSTEM.SQL.Shell()
SQL Command Line Shell
----------------------------------------------------

The command prefix is currently set to: <<nothing>>.
Enter q to quit, ? for help.
USER>>Select * from SLastName.Person
1.      Select * from SLastName.Person

ID      City    DOB     Name    Sex     State   Street  Zip
1                       Dover, Ben
2                       Dover, Ilene
3                       Dover, Fred
4       Albany  35725   Hertz,Jules B.  M       NV      2950 Second Blvd47514
5       Gansevoort      43013   Ott,Keith O.    F       SD      4351 Elm Drive64
730
6       Boston  37038   Avery,Juanita U.        F       WY      7450 Main Avenue
80125
7       Ukiah   34175   Hanson,Alfred K.        M       MS      3381 Washington
Drive   68629
8       Reston  33054   West,Chris T.   M       KY      9139 Clinton Drive39679
9       Elmhurst        56437   Ingersol,Aviel K.       M       AZ      5189 Map
le Place        17591
```

The data returned on your system will be different than mine because the data generated is random. This is only one way to invoke SQL with your data.

Common sense and a sense of humor is the same thing, moving at different speeds.

A sense of humor is just common sense, dancing –

William James.

Huh?

Chapter 15 - Atelier Properties

> This chapter is for working in Atelier, the chapters for working in Atelier are 11, 13, 15, and 17.

ALastName.Person

In this chapter we will modify an Object Class in Atelier.

The Class name we will use is *ALastName.Person*.

> The A is for Atelier,
>
> LastName is for your last name, and
>
> Person is for "Person".

My last name is Kadow, so the Class name I would use is *AKADOW.PERSON*.

This is to avoid confusion later and to identify your classes in case others on your system are going through the same book.

Atelier Properties for Class ALastName.Person

Now we are going to add a few more properties to the ALastName.Person Class.

Here is a list of the properties we are adding:

- DOB and DOBIndex, (date of birth)
- Sex, (M/F)
- Street address
- City and CityIndex,
- State and StateIndex,
- Zip and ZipIndex.

Add the new lines on the next page.

```
Person.cls ⊠
1⊖ Class ALastName.Person Extends (%Persistent,%Library.Populate,%XML.Adaptor)
2  {
3
4  Property Name As %Name(POPSPEC = "Name()") [Required ];
5
6  Index NameIndex On Name;
7
8  Property DOB As %Date(POPSPEC = "Date()") [ Required ];
9
10  Index DOBIndex On DOB;
11
12  Property Sex As %String(DISPLAYLIST = ",Male,Female", VALUELIST = ",M,F") [ Required ];
13
14  Index SexIndex On Sex;
15
16  Property Street As %String(POPSPEC = "Street()") [ Required ];
17
18  Property City As %String(POPORDER = "City()") [ Required ];
19
20  Index CityIndex On City;
21
22  Property State As %String(POPSPEC = "USState()") [ Required ];
23
24  Index StateIndex On State;
25
26  Property Zip As %String(POPSPEC = "USZip()") [ Required ];
27
28  Index ZipIndex On Zip;
29
```

Data Population

InterSystems built into Caché some utility applications. One of these is the *Populate Utility*. It is one of their better ideas.

Data population is where dummy data or test data fills up your database, as much as you specify.

Many of the data types have this capability, like name, date, street, city, ssn, etc. And even those data types that do not have this capability, you can build it in yourself with a little extra coding.

Look at your class and all the properties that have the POPSPEC parameter. We are now going to use the POPSPEC parameter to add dummy data to your database.

Populate Documentation

From the Caché Cube in the system tray, select Documentation. Then Search for *Populate*.

Or use the link *http://doc.intersystems.com/* , select the version of documentation you want, and search from there.

Populate the Class

Now that you have included %Populate in the Class Extends statement and set up the POPSPEC parameters, all you have to do is issue the following command in the Caché Terminal

```
Cache TRM:14192 (TRYCACHE)

File   Edit   Help


Node: PMKADOW, Instance: TRYCACHE


Username: pmkad
Password: ***
USER>

USER>Write ##class(ALastName.Person).Populate(100)
100
USER>
```

So, with one command, we can create 100 or more instances or objects of your class, very cool!

Now you can run SQL and see all the data it returns.

Using SQL to see your data

From the Caché Cube in your system tray, select *Terminal*.

Type in the commands from the following example.

As you can see IDs 1,2,3 are for Ben, Ilene and Fred Dover we added initially. For the rest of the IDs through 100 all have full data.

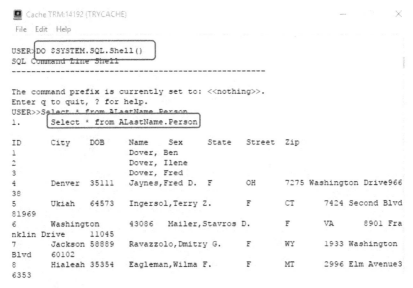

The data returned on your system will be different than mine because the data generated is random. This is only one way to invoke SQL with your data.

Chapter 16 - Studio Methods

> This chapter is for working in Studio, the chapters for working in Studio are 10, 12, 14, and 16.

SLastName.Person

In this chapter we will modify an Object Class in Studio.

The Class name we will use is *SLastName.Person.*

>> The S is for Studio,

>> LastName is for your last name, and

>> Person is for "Person".

My last name is Kadow, so the Class name I would use is *SKADOW.PERSON.*

This is to avoid confusion later and to identify your classes in case others on your system are going through the same book.

Studio Methods for Class SLastName.Person

So far, we created a Class, added Properties. Then after adding some data we instantiated the Class, next we displayed our data with the SQL Shell. Now we are going to look at Methods.
As you remember, Methods are the code that acts on our data within the class.

There are two types of Methods.

> ➤ Instance Method
> ➤ Class Method

Instance Method

An Instance Method must be based on an Oref (Object Reference).

Insert the code in the lines from the next example after the ZipIndex line of the SLastName.Person Class.

```
Index ZipIndex On Zip;

Method AddData(inName As %Name, inDOB As %Date,
inSex As %String, inStreet As %String,
inCity As %String, inState As %String, inZip As %String)
{
        Set ..Name   = inName
        Set ..DOB    = inDOB
        Set ..Sex    = inSex
        Set ..Street = inStreet
        Set ..City   = inCity
        Set ..State  = inState
        Set ..Zip    = inZip
}
```

Invoking a Class Method

I have covered this before but thought it good to cover it again.

In native Caché and MUMPS, the traditional way to invoke an executable procedure is with a DO, or DO While or sometimes with a $, or $$, or Call or even $$$ for a Macro.

In Object Technology the syntax to execute a Class Method within a Class is:

Set Oref=##class(Package.ClassName).%Method(Param)

Where:

- **Oref** – an Oref represents an Object Reference. What this means is that this is the result from calling an Executable Procedure of a Class. The output from calling this class is placed in the variable "Oref". Another way to think of an Oref is that it is an "in-memory" representation of the Class. This class typically contains data and executable procedures.
- **##class** – Object Technology "call" which invokes this method within this class
- **Package** – package or schema part of the class name
- **ClassName** – just that, the "Class Name"
- **%Method** – "Class Method" within the class
- **Param** – any parameters being passed

Invoking a Method

To invoke a Method, as opposed to a Class Method, that class need to be already instantiated, or already "in-memory."

> Set Oref=##class(Package.ClassName).%New()

>> To create a new empty Oref of the Class based on the %New executable. For a definition of Oref see the previous page.

>> Now that we have an new empty Oref (Object Reference) of the Class, we can make calls into the Class.

> Do Oref.Method(param)

>> Here we call the Method of the Oref Class passing it whatever parameters are necessary.

> Or

> Write Oref.Method(param) – if the method returns a value

> Set X=Oref.Method(param) – if the method returns a value

>> Here we call the Method and accept whatever value the Method passes back.

Run an Instance Method

Now to run this Instance Method, bring up the *Terminal* from the Caché Cube and enter the following commands.

```
USER>Set Name="Volt, John"

USER>Set Dob=$ZDATEH("11/05/1980")

USER>Set Sex="M"

USER>Set St="100 Main"

USER>Set City="Evans City"

USER>Set State="PA"

USER>Set Zip="16001"

USER>

USER>Set Oref=##class(SLastName.Person).%New()

USER>Do Oref.AddData(Name,Dob,Sex,St,City,State,Zip)

USER>

USER>Set Stat = Oref.%Save()

USER>

USER>If Stat '= 1 W $SYSTEM.OBJ.DisplayError(Stat)

USER>Write Stat
1
USER>
```

In this example, we set a number of variables (Name, Dob, Sex, Street, City, State, and Zip). Then we created a new empty Oref for the LastName.Person class.

As previously said, an Instance Method can only be run based on an Oref, so here we are creating an Oref to run this method.

Next, we do our *AddData* method passing in our variables.

Then we do our *%Save* method and check the return code by calling $SYSTEM.OBJ.DisplayError if the Stat is not one.

Now, just to be sure our add took, here is a SQL Query for John Volt.

```
USER>Do $SYSTEM.SQL.Shell()
SQL Command Line Shell
----------------------------------------------------

The command prefix is currently set to: <<nothing>>.
Enter q to quit, ? for help.
USER>>Select * from SLastName.Person where Name='Volt, John'
1.      Select * from SLastName.Person where Name='Volt, John'

ID      City    DOB     Name    Sex     State   Street  Zip
104     Evans City      51078   Volt, John      M       PA

1 Rows(s) Affected
statement prepare time(s)/globals/lines/disk: 0.1096s/54673/3537
          execute time(s)/globals/lines/disk: 0.0012s/20/1299/1n
                          cached query class: %sqlcq.USER.cls6
----------------------------------------------------
USER>>
```

Class Method

As we have seen, the Instance Method is based on an Oref, however a Class Method needs no Oref.

Class Methods may be used for the following purposes:

- To initially define an Oref
- Code that will affect multiple Object Instances
- A utility type of Method, like math calculations or date/time
- Any sort of processing that is not directly tied to a class's data

```
SLastName.Utility.cls

   Class SLastName.Utility Extends %Persistent
   {

ClassMethod Hello(Who)
   {
       If $G(Who)="" Set Who="World"
       Quit "Hello "_Who
   }
```

Here is a very simple Class Method that accepts an input parameter and says hello to the name in the parameter.

Bring up the Terminal from the Caché Cube and enter the following commands to execute this Class Method.

```
USER>Write ##class(SLastName.Utility).Hello()
Hello World
USER>

USER>W ##class(SLastName.Utility).Hello("Fred")
Hello Fred
USER>
```

Studio Sections

While in Studio it is necessary to get a wider understanding of how Studio works. (from Inside the Science of Fictional Treknology).

Alt+1 – Inspector

> The Inspector allows you to *Inspect* the Class Members (see chapter 16). The Class Members are: Property, Member, Query, Parameter, Index, Trigger, Storage, Foreign Key, Projection, and XData.

Alt+2 – Output from the code. This displays output generated

from the code itself.

Alt+3 – Workspace

> This is like a mini control section of the Classes, Windows and Namespaces of the Class and other parts.

Alt+4 – Storage

> This is a complicated part of Caché Studio that is mostly beyond the scope of this book. See Storage in Chapter 16.

Chapter 17 - Atelier Methods

> This chapter is for working in Atelier, the chapters for working in Atelier are 11, 13, 15, and 17.

ALastName.Person

In this chapter we will modify an Object Class in Atelier.

The Class name we will use is *ALastName.Person.*

> The A is for Atelier,
>
> LastName is for your last name, and
>
> Person is for "Person".

My last name is Kadow, so the Class name I would use is *AKADOW.PERSON.*

This is to avoid confusion later and to identify your classes in case others on your system are going through the same book.

Atelier Methods for Class ALastName.Person

So far, we created a Class, added Properties. Then after adding some data we instantiated the Class, next we displayed our data with the SQL Shell. Now we are going to look at Methods.
As you remember, Methods are the code that acts on our data within the class.

There are two types of Methods.
  ➢ Instance Method
  ➢ Class Method

Instance Method

An Instance Method must be based on an Oref (Object Reference).

Insert the code in the lines from the next example after the ZipIndex line of the ALastName.Person Class.

```
Index ZipIndex On Zip;
Method AddData(inName As %Name, inDOB As %Date,
inSex As %String, inStreet As %String,
inCity As %String, inState As %String, inZip As %String)
{
    Set ..Name   = inName
    Set ..DOB    = inDOB
    Set ..Sex    = inSex
    Set ..Street = inStreet
    Set ..City   = inCity
    Set ..State  = inState
    Set ..Zip    = inZip
}
```

Invoking a Class Method

In native Caché and MUMPS, the traditional way to invoke an executable procedure is with a DO, or DO While or sometimes with a $, or $$, or Call or even $$$ for a Macro.

In Object Technology the syntax to execute a Class Method within a Class is:

Set Oref=##class(Package.ClassName).%Method(Param)

Where:

- **Oref** – an Oref represents an Object Reference. What this means is that this is the result from calling an Executable Procedure of a Class. The output from calling this class is placed in the variable "Oref". Another way to think of an Oref is that it is an "in-memory" representation of the Class. This class typically contains data and executable procedures.
- **##class** – Object Technology "call" which invokes this method within this class
- **Package** – package or schema part of the class name
- **ClassName** – just that, the "Class Name"
- **%Method** – "Class Method" within the class
- **Param** – any parameters being passed

Invoking a Method

To invoke a Method, as opposed to a Class Method, that class need to be already instantiated, or already "in-memory."

> Set Oref=##class(Package.ClassName).%New()

>> To create a new empty Oref of the Class based on the %New executable. For a definition of Oref see the previous page.

>> Now that we have an new empty Oref (Object Reference) of the Class, we can make calls into the Class.

> Do Oref.Method(param)

>> Here we call the Method of the Oref Class passing it whatever parameters are necessary.

> Or

> Write Oref.Method(param) – if the method returns a value

> Set X=Oref.Method(param) – if the method returns a value

>> Here we call the Method and accept whatever value the Method passes back.

Run an Instance Method

Now to run this Instance Method, bring up the *Terminal* from the Caché Cube and enter the following commands.

```
USER>Set Name="Volt, John"

USER>Set Dob=$ZDATEH("11/05/1980")

USER>Set Sex="M"

USER>Set St="100 Main"

USER>Set City="Evans City"

USER>Set State="PA"

USER>Set Zip="16001"

USER>

USER>Set Oref=##class(ALastName.Person).%New()

USER>Do Oref.AddData(Name,Dob,Sex,St,City,State,Zip)

USER>

USER>Set Stat = Oref.%Save()

USER>

USER>If Stat '= 1 W $SYSTEM.OBJ.DisplayError(Stat)

USER>Write Stat
1
USER>
```

In this example, we set a number of variables (Name, Dob, Sex, State, City, State, and Zip). Then we created a new empty Oref for the LastName.Person class.

As previously said, an Instance Method can only be run based on an Oref, so here we are creating an Oref to run this method.

Next, we do our *AddData* method passing in our variables.

Then we do our *%Save* method and check the return code by calling $SYSTEM.OBJ.DisplayError if the Stat is not one.

Now, just to be sure out add took, here is a SQL Query for John Volt.

```
USER>Do $SYSTEM.SQL.Shell()
SQL Command Line Shell
-----------------------------------------------------------

The command prefix is currently set to: <<nothing>>.
Enter q to quit, ? for help.
USER>>Select * from ALastName.Person where Name='Volt, John'
2.      Select * from ALastName.Person where Name='Volt, John'

ID      City      DOB      Name      Sex      State    Street   Zip
104     Evans City         51078     Volt, John         M                 PA

1 Rows(s) Affected
statement prepare time(s)/globals/lines/disk: 0.0723s/54625/353·
          execute time(s)/globals/lines/disk: 0.0002s/3/1287/0m:
                        cached query class: %sqlcq.USER.cls7
-----------------------------------------------------------
```

Class Method

As we have seen, the Instance Method is based on an Oref, however a Class Method needs no Oref.

Class Methods may be used for the following purposes:

- To initially define an Oref
- Code that will affect multiple Object Instances
- A utility type of Method, like math calculations or date/time
- Any sort of processing that is not directly tied to a class's data

```
Person.cls        Utility.cls ⊠
  Class ALastName.Utility Extends %Persistent
  {

  ClassMethod Hello(Who)
  {
      If $G(Who)="" Set Who="World"
      Quit "Hello "_Who
  }
```

Here is a very simple Class Method that accepts an input parameter and says hello to the name in the parameter.

Bring up the Terminal from the Caché Cube and enter the following commands to execute this Class Method.

```
USER>Write ##class(ALastName.Utility).Hello()
Hello World
USER>

USER>Write ##class(ALastName.Utility).Hello("Fred")
Hello Fred
USER>
```

I've learned that people will forget what you said,

people will forget what you did,

but people will never forget how you made them feel –

Maya Angelou.

Chapter 18 - Class Members

Class Members

Within an Object Class there are the following Class Members:

- ➢ Properties – hold changeable data
  This is also called Class Properties
- ➢ Parameters – hold constant data
- ➢ Methods
  Two kinds of Methods:
    - − Instance Methods – based on Oref
    - − Class Methods – not based on Oref

- ➢ Queries
  Two kinds of Queries
    - − Basic Class Queries
    - − Custom Class Queries

- ➢ Indices
  Three kinds of Indices
    - − Standard
    - − BitMap
    - − BitSlice

- ➢ SQL Triggers
- ➢ Foreign Keys
- ➢ Storage
- ➢ Projections
- ➢ XData

Properties

The function of Properties is to hold data.

Properties may also be thought of as *fields*.

Properties define a number of different configurations and specifications. To describe them all is well beyond the scope of this book, for that, see the InterSystems documentation.

For help with Properties while in Caché Studio: Open the Inspector Window Alt+1.

For help with Properties while in Atelier: Help → Cheatsheet → Create an Atelier Class and then Add a Property. This allows you to use the Content Assist option.

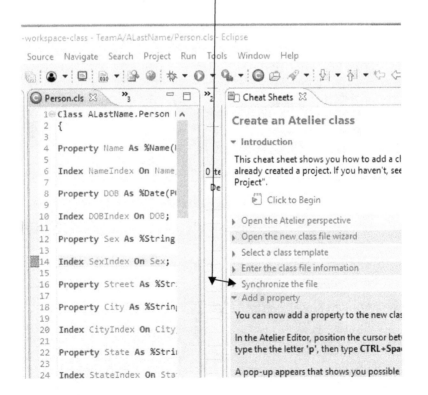

Properties using Outline View

The Outline View while in Atelier gives more information regarding Properties.

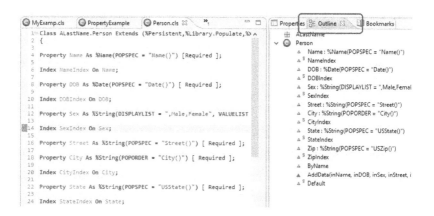

To find the Outline View, select the Windows Dropdown menu, then Show View and Outline. If Outline is not present you may need to go to Other . . . and find Outline there.

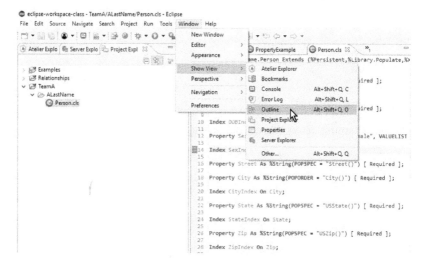

Property Keywords

Keywords can optionally be included in a property definition;

Required

When Required is specified, that property must hold some value before the instance is stored on disk.

InitialExpression

Specifies a first value for that property.

Transient

Specifies that the property is not stored in the database.

Private

These properties may only be accessed by the Class it belongs to and no outside class.

Calculated

These properties have no in-memory storage.

Age is a good example, it is calculated from the date of birth.

MultiDimensional

Specifies that the property is multidimensional.

Examples

I will demonstrate a few of the properties and show some of their wide-ranging functions and capabilities. The best way to do that is with examples.

Here are some examples:

➢ Integer property with an initial value of zero.

```
Property Count As %Integer [ InitialExpression = 0 ];
```

➢ String Property to hold a title with Max Length of 50 while using POPSPEC.

```
Property Title As %String(MAXLEN = 50, POPSPEC = "Title()");
```

➢ Date Property to hold a required date while using POPSPEC.

```
Property DOB As %Date(POPSPEC = "Date()") [ Required ]
```

➢ Integer Property to hold a Salary with a Max and Min Value.

```
Property Salary As %Integer(MAXVAL = 100000, MINVAL = 10000);
```

➢ Property to hold a string.

```
Property Status As %String(TRUNCATE = 1);
```

➢ String Property to hold an America Social Security number.

```
Property SSN As %String(PATTERN = "3N1""-""2N1""-""4N");
```

➢ Property to hold an address defined as a Class.

```
Home As SampleAddress
```

Here is the CLass Sample.Address

```
Class Sample.Address Extends (%SerialObject, %Populate,
%XML.Adaptor) [ StorageStrategy = AddressState ]
{
Property Street As %String(MAXLEN = 80, POPSPEC = "Street()");
Property City As %String(MAXLEN = 80, POPSPEC = "City()");
Property State As %String(MAXLEN = 2, POPSPEC = "USState()");
Property Zip As %String(MAXLEN = 5, POPSPEC = "USZip()");
}
```

Enumerated Properties

Meaning of the word *Enumerated*: a number of things, one by one.

Some properties have a ValueList and DisplayList parameters.

Here is an example of how ValueList and DisplayList work together using the LogicalToDisplay Method.

First, we define a Class with the property of Pets which has the parameters of ValueList and DisplayList.

```
Person.cls    Company.cls    Employee.cls    PropertyExample1.cls ⌧
1 Class SLastName.PropertyExample1 Extends %Persistent
2 {
3
4  Property Pets As %String(VALUELIST=",D,C,B",DISPLAYLIST=",Dogs,Cats,Birds");
5
```

Now we have a script that instantiates the PropertyExample1 Class. Next, we set Pets to "D" and then we display Pets using the LogicalToDisplay method, the resulting output string is "Dog". The LogicalToDisplay method is part of the %Persistent Class.

```
USER>Set Oref=##class(SLastName.PropertyExample1).%New()

USER>Set Oref.Pets = "D"

USER>Write Oref.PetsLogicalToDisplay(Oref.Pets)
Dogs
USER>
```

Parameters

A class parameter defines a constant value available to all objects of a given class.

- ➢ Parameter PARAMNAME;
- ➢ Parameter PARAMNAME as Type;
- ➢ Parameter PARAMNAME as Type = value;
- ➢ Parameter PARAMNAME as Type [Keywords] = value;

Parameter *types* include BOOLEAN, STRING, and INTEGER

Example:

```
Parameter ParamMsg As %String = "Message"
```

```
Parameter MaxValue As Integer = 5
```

Instance Method

An Instance Method must be based on an Oref (Object Reference).

This book demonstrates Instance Methods under Chapter 14 Studio Methods and Chapter 15 Atelier Methods

Class Method

A Class Method can just call a Method in a Class, it does not need to be based on an Oref.

This book demonstrates Class Methods under Chapter 14 Studio Methods and Chapter 15 Atelier Methods

Queries – Basic Class Query

I added a Basic Class Query to our ALastName.Person Class.

This is an example of a Basic Class Query for both Studio and Atelier.

```
Query ByName(Name As %String = "") As %SQLQuery
    (ROWSPEC="ID:%Integer,Name:%String,DOB:%Date")
    [ sqlName=ByName, SqlProc ]
    {
    SELECT ID, Name, DOB
    FROM ALastName.Person
    Where (Name %STARTSWITH :Name)
    ORDER BY Name
    }
```

I ran this query from the Caché Terminal

```
USER>Set statement=##class(%SQL.Statement).%New()

USER>Set status=statement.%PrepareClassQuery("ALastName.Person","ByName")

USER>If status'=1 {Do $system.OBJ.DisplayError(status) }

USER>Set resultset=statement.%Execute("A")

USER>While resultset.%Next() {Write !, resultset.%Get("Name")   }

Anderson,Kyra R.
Avery,Debra R.
USER>
```

As you remember we populated this Class back in chapter 11. This query asks for entries where the name begins with an A.

There is a *Custom Class Query* available but that is very advanced and not covered in this book.

Indices

An index optimizes data retrieval by storing a subset of data for each property. Indices may be created or deleted as needed

Indices may be one of the following:

- Standard
- BitMap
- BitSlice

Bitmap and Bitslice are very fast but have severe restrictions.

One of the traditional problems with Indices is keeping them updated and in sync with the actual data. Done properly, Caché Indices are self-populating and self-updating.

Based on the indices, the SQL Query is smart enough to know which Index to search first, second, etc. to ensure the most efficient lookup.

Indices were used in the ALastName.Person Class we already created.

```
 Person.cls ✕
  1  Class ALastName.Person Extends (%Persistent,%Library.Populate,%XML.Adaptor)
  2  {
  3
  4   Property Name As %Name(POPSPEC = "Name()") [Required ];
  5
  6   Index NameIndex On Name;
  7
  8   Property DOB As %Date(POPSPEC = "Date()") [ Required ];
  9
 10   Index DOBIndex On DOB;
 11
 12   Property Sex As %String(DISPLAYLIST = ",Male,Female", VALUELIST = ",M,F") [ Required ];
 13
 14   Index SexIndex On Sex;
 15
 16   Property Street As %String(POPSPEC = "Street()") [ Required ];
 17
 18   Property City As %String(POPORDER = "City()") [ Required ];
 19
```

One note, Indices do have some system overhead, do not create indices unless they are necessary.

SQL Trigger

A SQL Trigger specifies that upon an Event (Insert, Update or Delete) that some defined action should be taken.

Here is an example:

```
/// This trigger updates the Log
Trigger LogEvent [ Event = DELETE ]
{
    Set ProcessId = $SYSTEM.SYS.ProcessID()
    Set LogOref.Entry = "Delete - "_ProcessId

}
```

Storage

Specifies the type of storage to be used:

    (1) Caché Storage (default)

    (2) Caché SQL Storage

    (3) Custom Storage

The Storage section of a Class defines what and how a Global or Globals will be mapped to the Class. When you develop a Class from scratch, the Storage takes care of itself. However, when you develop a

Storage for a preexisting Global

If you have a preexisting Global that you want to create a Class for you need to use the Caché Studio tools to map the Global to the Class. This is not an exercise for the faint of heart, if you have never done this before I suggest getting help from InterSystems' Worldwide Support Center.

> InterSystems' Worldwide Support Center
>
> Telephone: +1 617 621–0700
>
> Fax: +1 617 374–9391
>
> Email: support@InterSystems.com
>
> Website: *http://www.InterSystems.com*

When developing a class, you may add and delete or re–add properties. Be aware that the storage of a class will maintain all properties added since its inception. This is done to maintain Global integrity.

Mapping Globals to Classes

There are several excellent articles on the very difficult art of mapping existing Globals to Classes in the Developer Community.

See the links below.

https://community.intersystems.com/post/art-mapping-globals-classes-1-3

https://community.intersystems.com/post/art-mapping-globals-classes%C2%A0-2-3

https://community.intersystems.com/post/art-mapping-globals-classes-3-3

https://community.intersystems.com/post/art-mapping-globals-classes-4-3

https://community.intersystems.com/post/art-mapping-globals-classes-5-3

Many thanks to Brendan Bannon the author of the above posts on mapping Globals classes.

Used with permission.

Regenerate a clean Storage

When you are finished developing your class you should delete the storage and then regenerate it.

If you want the class compiler to generate a clean storage structure, delete the class' storage definition and recompile the class.

You can do this as follows:

➢ Open the class in Caché Studio.

➢ Right–click on the default Storage definition in the Class Inspector. If the Inspector is not visible, bring it up using Alt+1. Ensure Storage is visible in the left window. Invoke the Delete command in the popup menu.

➢ Compile the class. This will cause the class compiler to generate a new storage definition for the class.

Projections

Class projections extend the behavior of the class compiler. It provides methods to generate additional code when a class is compiled. These methods are used by Java and C++.

XData

A class member that holds a named block of well–formed XML structured data, it is typically used with Ensemble or Zen classes.

Chapter 19 - Relationships: One to Many

One of the aims of Object Technology is to simulate the real world with computer systems.

Relationships

We have Relationships in the real world.

There are many ways that Relationships can be simulated with computer systems, one to one, arrays, lists, and so on, each has its advantages and disadvantages.

Some of the real-world relationships are:

➢ Marriage partner relationship,

➢ Parents to children relationship,

➢ Relationship between Invoice and line items,

➢ Street to houses relationship,

➢ Book to pages relationship,

➢ Employer to employee relationship,

➢ etc., etc., etc., the examples abound!

In prior chapters, we created a class, added elements to it and then instantiated the class which gave us an object.

In this chapter, we will look at how Caché defines Relationships, specifically a *One to Many* type of Relationships.

There are other types of relationships: Parent to Child, Many to Many and so on. Once you understand the basics of One to Many Relationships, you should be able to create the other types

I am not going to go back and forth between Studio and Atelier, I am only going to use Atelier as an example. The Studio version of it will be almost the same.

I will however use the same naming convention I established in the previous chapters for Atelier.

Relationships Guidelines

1) A relationship is an association between two persistent objects, tied together with each object's unique property.
2) Relationships must exist between persistent classes, actually between two properties.
3) Relationships are binary, they can only be between two classes, or a class and itself.
4) Both sides or properties of the relationship must point to the other.
5) A relationship is bidirectional, functioning in two directions at the same time. If you update the value of the relationship property on one side, the other side is changed.

Caché Relationships

A relationship is an association between two persistent objects, each object must have a relationship property, which defines its half of the relationship.

Caché allows two types of Relationships:

> **Parent to Child Relationship:**
>> o A Child is tied to a Parent, if the Parent is removed, the Child is also deleted.
>>
>> o Once associated with a Parent, the Child can never be associated with a different Parent
>>
>> o The Parent and Child Classes are linked at compile time.

> **One to Many Relationship**
>> o The "One" Class and "Many" Class have none of the restrictions of the Parent to Child Relationship.

One to Many Relationship

In this chapter, we are going to create a Company Class, which will serve as our *One* Class. Next, we will create an Employee Class which will serve as our *Many* Class.

So, we have One Company with many employees.

This concept can be carried further, the Company Class could have all car manufacturers companies. So, as we step back we start to see a hierarchy develop using the One to Many structure.

While in Atelier, under a Project name called *Relationships*, create the Company Class and Employee Class as shown below.

Company Class

```
Person.cls      *Company.cls      Employee.cls
1  Class ALastName.Company Extends (%Persistent,%Library.Populate,%XML.Adaptor)
2  {
3  Property CompanyName As %String [ Required ];
4
5  Index CompanyNameIndex On CompanyName [ Unique ];
6
7  Relationship LinkToEmployee As ALastName.Employee
8  [ Cardinality = many, Inverse = LinkToCompany ];
9
```

Employee Class

```
 Person.cls      "Company.cls      "Employee.cls ☒
1  Class ALastName.Employee Extends (%Persistent,%Library.Populate,%XML.Adaptor)
2  {
3  Property EmployeeName As %String [ Required ];
4
5  Index EmployeeNameIndex On EmployeeName [ Unique ];
6
7  Relationship LinkToCompany As ALastName.Company
8  [ Cardinality = one, Inverse = LinkToEmployee ];
9
```

Note, you will not get an error free compile until both Classes are created. This is because the two Relationship properties, *LinkToEmployee* and *LinkToCompany* depend upon and need each other.

Before we go further, we need to take a closer look at the two Relationship properties and see how they complement each other.

I know this table is complicated, but it is imperative that all connections are made correctly, or your relationships will not work.

ALastName.Company	ALastName.Employee
Relationship LinkToEmployee	Relationship LinkToCompany
As LastName.Employee	As LastName.Company
[Cardinality = many,	[Cardinality = one,
Inverse = LinkToCompany];	Inverse = LinkToEmployee];

The Relationship properties are for linking the two Classes (via the properties) together.

The cardinality defines the cardinality **of the other side** of the relationship.

The cardinality can be *one*, *many*, *parent*, or *children*. If one side is *parent*, the other side is *children*. If one side is *many*, the other side is *one*.

The inverse property **is the other classes's** Relationship.

Follow the above closely, it is easy to become confused.

Use descriptive words like *LinkToEmployee* and *LinkToParent* to avoid confusion.

One final note, the two Relationship Properties, *LinkToEmployee* and *LinkToParent* do not carry or contain any data, they are for the purpose of connecting the two Classes together, and this is their *only* purpose.

Delete Data

This example shows you how to delete all your data concerning Relationships and start over, if it comes to that. In my experience, it has come to that many times.

```
USER>; These next four lines are included in

USER> ; case you need to run this example again.

USER> ; They delete the Globals that this

USER> ; sequence of commands create.

USER>

USER>Kill ^ALastName.CompanyD

USER>Kill ^ALastName.CompanyI

USER>Kill ^ALastName.EmployeeD

USER>Kill ^ALastName.EmployeeI
```

Create a new Company

Here we will create a new company. The new company's Oref is just "C", remember an Oref is just a variable to MUMPS. Then we set the company's name and then save the company to the database.

```
USER> ; create a new Company Oref

USER> Set C=##class(ALastName.Company).%New()

USER>

USER> ; populate the Company Oref with data

USER> Set C.CompanyName = "AJAX NEW WIDGETS"

USER>

USER> ; save company information

USER> Write C.%Save()
1
USER>

USER> Write C.%Id() ; Write Company ID
1
USER>
```

Create 3 new Employees

In this next block of text script:

We use the ALastName.Employee Class to create 3 empty employees. The Orefs of the 3 Classes are E1, E2, and E3 respectively.

Next, we add the name of Larry, Moe, and Curly Joe to our 3 employee classes.

Then we save the 3 classes and lastly, we display the IDs of the 3 classes to be used later.

```
USER> ; create 3 new Employees

USER>Set E1=##class(ALastName.Employee).%New()

USER>Set E2=##class(ALastName.Employee).%New()

USER>Set E3=##class(ALastName.Employee).%New()

USER> ; populate the 3 new Employees with names

USER>Set E1.EmployeeName = "Larry"

USER>Set E2.EmployeeName = "Moe"

USER>Set E3.EmployeeName = "Curly Joe"

USER> ; save the 3 new Employees

USER>Write E1.%Save()
1
USER>Write E2.%Save()
1
USER>Write E3.%Save()
1
USER>Write E1.%Id()
1
USER>Write E2.%Id()
2
USER>Write E3.%Id()
3
```

Establish a Link - Company (One), Employee (Many)

Now we will link the Company Object and 3 Employee Objects together.

Unlike Parent and Child Relationships, with *OneToMany* Relationships we can create companies and Employees and link or unlink them at will.

To link the Company and Employees together we need their IDs. You may remember the ID, but then again, you may not. To see the IDs of the Company and Employees we will use SQL.

Use SQL to find IDs of the Company & Employees

From the Caché Cube in your system tray, select *Terminal*.

Please consider the following examples.

```
USER>do $SYSTEM.SQL.Shell()
SQL Command Line Shell
------------------------------------------------------

The command prefix is currently set to: <<nothing>>.
Enter q to quit, ? for help.
USER>>Select * from ALastName.Company
1.      Select * from ALastName.Company

ID      CompanyName
1       AJAX NEW WIDGETS

1 Rows(s) Affected
statement prepare time(s)/globals/lines/disk: 0.0276s/64/604/22ms
            execute time(s)/globals/lines/disk: 0.0021s/25/506/4ms
                        cached query class: %sqlcq.USER.cls8
------------------------------------------------------
USER>>Select * from ALastName.Employee
2.      Select * from ALastName.Employee

ID      EmployeeName    LinkToCompany
1       Larry
2       Moe
3       Curly Joe

3 Rows(s) Affected
statement prepare time(s)/globals/lines/disk: 0.0118s/24/598/13ms
            execute time(s)/globals/lines/disk: 0.0001s/4/779/0ms
                        cached query class: %sqlcq.USER.cls9
------------------------------------------------------
USER>>
```

From the example above, we can see that the ID of the Company is 1. The IDs from the three Employees are 1,2, and 3 respectively.

The next step is to bring the Company and the three Employees into memory in preparation for linking.

Bring the Company and three Employees into memory.

```
USER>Set C=##class(ALastName.Company).%OpenId(1)

USER>Set E1=##class(ALastName.Employee).%OpenId(1)

USER>Set E2=##class(ALastName.Employee).%OpenId(2)

USER>Set E3=##class(ALastName.Employee).%OpenId(3)
```

Now that the Company and three Employees are in-memory we can link them together.

Link the Company and three Employees.

```
USER>Do C.LinkToEmployee.Insert(E1)

USER>Do C.LinkToEmployee.Insert(E2)

USER>Do C.LinkToEmployee.Insert(E3)

USER>Set Stat=C.%Save()      ; Save all links

USER>If Stat'=1 W $SYSTEM.OBJ.DisplayError(Status)

USER>

USER>; the following 4 calls validates that the

USER>; Orefs are valid. Each call should

USER>; return a 1. This call ($Isobject)

USER>; ensure the Orefs in an object

USER>

USER>Write $Isobject(C)
1
USER>Write $Isobject(E1)
1
USER>Write $Isobject(E2)
1
USER>Write $Isobject(E3)
1
USER>
```

Display a Relationship with SQL

In this next example, we are going to use the SQL Shell to display the Company, Employee, and their Relationship. The SQL Shell displays ">>" as a prompt.

```
USER>DO $SYSTEM.SQL.Shell()
SQL Command Line Shell
------------------------------------------------------

The command prefix is currently set to: <<nothing>>.
Enter q to quit, ? for help.
USER>>Select * from ALastName.Company
1.      Select * from ALastName.Company

ID      CompanyName
1       AJAX NEW WIDGETS

1 Rows(s) Affected
statement prepare time(s)/globals/lines/disk: 0.0293s/66/602/20ms
          execute time(s)/globals/lines/disk: 0.0022s/25/506/2ms
                             cached query class: %sqlcq.USER.cls8
------------------------------------------------------
USER>>Select * from ALastName.Employee
2.      Select * from ALastName.Employee

ID      EmployeeName    LinkToCompany
1       Larry     1
2       Moe       1
3       Curly Joe      [1]

3 Rows(s) Affected
statement prepare time(s)/globals/lines/disk: 0.0162s/40/603/16ms
          execute time(s)/globals/lines/disk: 0.0009s/4/781/0ms
                             cached query class: %sqlcq.USER.cls9
------------------------------------------------------
```

From the Company's side there is no sign that the Company is in a relationship. From the Employee's side however, we do see a LinkToCompany's column with the Company's ID that we are linked to.

Remove a Relationship

Let say in the Company and Employees relationship we want to remove "Moe." As you remember Moe's ID was 2. If you do not remember Moe's ID you can always run a SQL Shell as we did before to find Moe's ID.

The command sequence to remove Moe from the relationship is as follows.

Using Moe's Oref, we set the LinkToCompany to null. That removes Moe's relationship to the Company.

```
USER>Set Oref=##class(ALastName.Employee).%OpenId(2)

USER>Set Oref.LinkToCompany=""

USER>Write Oref.%Save()
1
USER>
```

Remove Moe's link to the company. This is only possible in OneToMany relationships and not in ParentToChild relationships.

This is not a book that should be tossed lightly aside.

It should be hurled with great force –

Dorothy Parker.

Chapter 20 - Processing Relationships

This chapter will give examples of how you can process relationships in your code. These examples will use the *One to Many Relationship* we created in the previous chapter.

Iterate Company thru Employees

In this example we will iterate using a *One to Many Relationship*. However, if you remember we only added 3 employees and deleted one, but the process is still valid no matter how many employees we have.

Here is the code to go through all the Employees for our Company.

```
MyExamp.cls ⊠
 1  Class ALastName.MyExamp Extends %Persistent
 2  {
 3
 4  ClassMethod CompanyToEmployee()
 5  {
 6  /// ; Open the Company ID
 7  Set C=##class(ALastName.Company).%OpenId(1)
 8  Write C.CompanyName
 9
10  ; prime the EmpKey
11  Set EmpKey=""
12
13  Do {
14      Set Emp=C.LinkToEmployee.GetNext(.EmpKey)
15      If Emp'="" {
16          Write !,Emp.EmployeeName
17      }
18  } While EmpKey'=""
19  Quit 1
20
21  }
```

As you can see we used the Class Method *CompanyToEmployee*. We first opened the Companies Oref and assigned it to the "C" variable. Next, we wrote out the Company's name, "AJAX NEW WIDGETS".

We set the EmpKey to blank, this tells the upcoming loop to start at the beginning.

The first thing we do when we enter the loop is to get the next Employee based on EmpKey. We place the Object in the Emp Oref. Then, we write out the Employee name from the Emp Oref only if Emp is not blank.

We continue to get the next Employee and write out the name until the Emp Oref is blank, at that point we quit and pass back a 1 which indicate success.

From the Terminal, here is the code to run our Method and see our output, Larry and Curly Joe.

```
USER>S ReturnCode=##class(ALastName.MyExamp).CompanyToEmployee()
AJAX NEW WIDGETS
Larry
Curly Joe
USER>
```

Display Company Name from Employee

In this example using the *One to Many* (Employees to Company) relationship we will write the Company Name based on the Employee relationship.

```
USER>Set Employee=##class(ALastName.Employee).%OpenId(1)

USER>Write !,Employee.EmployeeName

Larry
USER>

USER>Write !,Employee.LinkToCompany.CompanyName

AJAX NEW WIDGETS
USER>
```

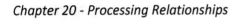

He was so narrow minded he could see through a keyhole with both eyes - Molly Ivins.

Chapter 21 - Inheritance

Object Technology Inheritance Description

In object-oriented programming, inheritance allows new objects to take on or inherit the properties of present or already existing objects.

A class that is the basis for inheritance is called a superclass or sometimes a base class.

A class that inherits from a superclass is called a subclass or a derived class.

If you think of it as a hierarchy, superclass is always above, and a subclass is always below. Obviously, the descriptions change once you introduce a third, fourth or more levels.

A superclass for one level may just be a subclass for another level, it all depends on where you are when you look at the other levels.

A good analogy is a corporation's organization chart. Who is above and who is below all depends on where you are.

Parent and Child Class

The terms *parent class* and *child class* can also be used. A child inherits properties and methods from its parent. A child may also add additional properties and methods of its own.

Using inheritance to make this hierarchy often creates a system that is easier to understand code, but most importantly, it allows you to reuse and organize code more effectively, or that is its aim.

Object Technology Inheritance exists in a hierarchy of classes where the more generalized classes are toward the top of the hierarchy and the specific and detailed ones are toward the bottom.

An Object Inherits properties or methods from the object above it. We have already seen this in your ALastName.Person Class when the %Save method was executed. The %Save method does not exist in your ALastName.Person class but did exist in the %Persistent class.

Object Technology Inheritance works when one class/object has properties from two or more objects that are above it. Indeed, there may be many objects that contribute to making up one logical object.

Multiple Inheritance

Within Caché, one class can inherit properties and methods from multiple classes. This is what is known as *multiple inheritance.*

Designing an Object Technology based system

Designing a system within Object Technology using multiple interrelated classes and inheritance is certainly a challenging and demanding task. The designers need to spend concentrated planning sessions at the beginning of the project. This is especially true with an eye for the future.

The more time and energy put into front-end planning has never been so true as with designing an object technology based system that uses inheritance. When front-end planning is skimped upon, the more and complex problems will occur as the project progresses. On the other side, when sufficient and even abundant effective front-end planning is done the less problems will occur as the project progresses.

But alas, managers and sponsors always want to see their projects start and move along as soon as possible. This always seems to be the rub.

It would help tremendously to have in attendance designers who have already gone through this process before as they can share what works and what does not as well as the pitfalls.

While building the Application, questions and problems will arise that will need input from the designers. Issues will come up that may not have been foreseen by the designers and may require modifications to the Application design. Resolving these issues as early as possible will prove much less costly then the alternative.

Inheritance allows the Properties and Methods of one class to be passed down the hierarchy structure to another class. This means less programming is needed. However, this can quickly become unmanageable.

Inheritance Application

Our Inheritance example will be very simple, but I hope you can understand some of the concepts with this example.

So far, we have created the ALastName.Person class in Chapter 11 and modified it in subsequent chapters. A display of it follows.

```
Person.cls ☒    PropertyExamples2.cls
1  Class ALastName.Person Extends (%Persistent,%Library.Populate,%XML.Adaptor)
2  {
3
4  Property Name As %Name(POPSPEC = "Name()") [Required ];
5
6  Index NameIndex On Name;
7
8  Property DOB As %Date(POPSPEC = "Date()") [ Required ];
9
10 Index DOBIndex On DOB;
11
12 Property Sex As %String(DISPLAYLIST = ",Male,Female", VALUELIST = ",M,F") [ Required ];
13
14 Index SexIndex On Sex;
15
16 Property Street As %String(POPSPEC = "Street()") [ Required ];
17
18 Property City As %String(POPORDER = "City()") [ Required ];
19
20 Index CityIndex On City;
21
22 Property State As %String(POPSPEC = "USState()") [ Required ];
23
24 Index StateIndex On State;
25
26 Property Zip As %String(POPSPEC = "USZip()") [ Required ];
27
28 Index ZipIndex On Zip;
29
30 Query ByName(Name As %String = "") As %SQLQuery
31     (ROWSPEC="ID:%Integer,Name:%String,DOB:%Date")
32     [ sqlName=ByName, SqlProc ]
33     {
34     SELECT ID, Name, DOB
35     FROM ALastName.Person
36     Where (Name %STARTSWITH :Name)
37     ORDER BY Name
38     }
39
```

We have also created the ALastName.Employee class in Chapter 17. A display of this class follows.

```
Person.cls        PropertyExamples2.cls      Employee.cls
1  Class ALastName.Employee Extends (%Persistent,%Library.Populate,%XML.Adaptor)
2  {
3  Property EmployeeName As %String [ Required ];
4
5  Index EmployeeNameIndex On EmployeeName [ Unique ];
6
7  Relationship LinkToCompany As ALastName.Company
8  [ Cardinality = one, Inverse = LinkToEmployee ];
9
```

What we are going to do is make the A.LastName.Employee class Extend from the ALastName.Person Class.

This should allow all properties and methods in the ALastName.Person class be available to the A.LastName.Employee class.

Make the following modification to the A.LastName.Employee class.

The text you should add is ",ALastName.Person"

```
Person.cls        PropertyExamples2.cls      *Employee.cls
1  Class ALastName.Employee Extends (%Persistent,%Library.Populate,%XML.Adaptor,ALastName.Person)
2  {
3  Property EmployeeName As %String [ Required ];
4
5  Index EmployeeNameIndex On EmployeeName [ Unique ];
6
7  Relationship LinkToCompany As ALastName.Company
8  [ Cardinality = one, Inverse = LinkToEmployee ];
9
```

After you make the modification above and save your file, you should see that the following storage data items are added to the ALastName.Employee class.

```
 Person.cls      PropertyExamples2.cls      Employee.cls

 1  Class ALastName.Employee Extends (%Persistent,%Library.Populate,%
 2  {
 3  Property EmployeeName As %String [ Required ];
 4
 5  Index EmployeeNameIndex On EmployeeName [ Unique ];
 6
 7  Relationship LinkToCompany As ALastName.Company
 8  [ Cardinality = one, Inverse = LinkToEmployee ];
 9
10  Storage Default
11  {
12  <Data name="EmployeeDefaultData">
13  <Value name="1">
14  <Value>%%CLASSNAME</Value>
15  </Value>
16  <Value name="2">
17  <Value>EmployeeName</Value>
18  </Value>
19  <Value name="3">
20  <Value>LinkToCompany</Value>
21  </Value>
22  <Value name="4">
23  <Value>Name</Value>
24  </Value>
25  <Value name="5">
26  <Value>DOB</Value>
27  </Value>
28  <Value name="6">
29  <Value>Sex</Value>
30  </Value>
31  <Value name="7">
32  <Value>Street</Value>
33  </Value>
34  <Value name="8">
35  <Value>City</Value>
36  </Value>
37  <Value name="9">
38  <Value>State</Value>
39  </Value>
40  <Value name="10">
```

Next let's instantiate the *Curly Joe* object while in the Terminal. If you remember *Curly Joe* has an ID of 3.

```
USER>Set Oref=##class(ALastName.Employee).%OpenId(3)

USER>zw Oref
Oref=<OBJECT REFERENCE>[1@ALastName.Employee]
+----------------- general information ---------------
|        oref value: 1
|        class name: ALastName.Employee
|            %%OID: $lb("3","ALastName.Employee")
| reference count: 2
+----------------- attribute values ------------------
|        %Concurrency = 1  <Set>
|               City = ""
|                DOB = ""
|       EmployeeName = "Curly Joe"
|               Name = ""
|                Sex = ""
|              State = ""
|             Street = ""
|                Zip = ""
+----------------- swizzled references ---------------
|     i%LinkToCompany = 1  <Set>
|     r%LinkToCompany = ""  <Set>
+----------------------------------------------------

USER>
```

As you can see *Curly Joe* has all the attributes that the Person class has. *Curly Joe* has *inherited* these attributes.

Let us execute the AddData Instance Method which is now available to the ALastName.Employee Class.

```
USER>Set Dob=$ZDATEH("05/01/1970")

USER>Set Sex="M"

USER>Set St="508 Pershing Ave"

USER>Set City="Worcester"

USER>Set State="MA"

USER>Set Zip="01752"

USER>Set Name="Curley Joe"

USER>Do Oref.AddData(Name,Dob,Sex,St,City,State,Zip)

USER>Write Oref.%Save()
1
USER>
```

Using the ALastName.Exmployee Class we have executed the AddData Instance Method to add Curly Joe's data.

Next, we use SQL to display the data we just added to Curly Joe's ALastName.Emplyee Class.

```
USER>Do $SYSTEM.SQL.Shell()
SQL Command Line Shell
-----------------------------------------------------

The command prefix is currently set to: <<nothing>>.
Enter q to quit, ? for help.
USER>>Select * from ALastName.Employee
1.      Select * from ALastName.Employee

ID      City    DOB     EmployeeName    LinkToCompany   Name    Sex     States
eet     Zip
1                       Larry   1
2                       Moe
3       Worcester       47237   Curly Joe       1       Curley Joe      MMA508
ershing Ave     01752

3 Rows(s) Affected
statement prepare time(s)/globals/lines/disk: 0.2421s/56679/340791/162ms
        execute time(s)/globals/lines/disk: 0.0020s/27/1796/2ms
                cached query class: %sqlcq.USER.cls9
```

$SYSTEM.OBJ.DisplayError

I would like to take this one step further. Suppose we made a mistake and entered a bogus date.

When we executed the %Save method it returned an error, but who can figure out what the error is.

As shown below, we can use the $SYSTEM.OBJ.DisplayError to get a clear picture of the error.

```
USER>Set Dob=$ZDATE("")

USER>w Dob
12/31/1840
USER>

USER>Do Oref.AddData(Name,Dob,Sex,St,City,State,Zip)

USER>Write Oref.%Save()
0 \▯'
        12/31/1840Ô"zDOBIsValid+1^ALastName.Person.1▯USERªᵉe^zDOBIsValid+1^ALastN
ame.Person.1^1,e^%ValidateObject+6^ALastName.Employee.1^2-e^%SerializeObject+3^.
LastName.Employee.1^1"e^%Save+8^ALastName.Employee.1^5e^^^0p0 1▯ª▯ALastName.Em
ployee:DOB
        12/31/1840<▯EmbedErr+1^%occSystem▯USER^EmbedErr+1^%occSystem^1
USER>Set Status=Oref.%Save()

USER>Write $SYSTEM.OBJ.DisplayError(Status)
ERROR #7207: Datatype value '12/31/1840' is not a valid number
    > ERROR #5002: Datatype validation failed on property 'ALastName.Employee:DOB
, with value equal to "12/31/1840"1
USER>
```

Appendix A - Migration to Atelier

Moving your code from Caché Studio to Atelier is not as easy as it may seem. It will take some planning.

First and foremost make a good backup copy of your code from Caché Studio.

There is a very good article on migrating your code, so I will not replicate the process.

From the Workbench → Help → Help Contents → Search for → *Managing Migration to Atelier.*

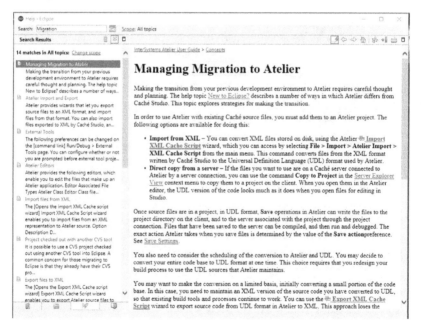

*Even if you're on the right track, you'll get run over if you
just sit there – Will Rogers.*

Appendix B – Automatic Software Update

It is a good idea to turn on the automatic software update to ensure you are always running the most recent version of Atelier.

From your Workbench, select the Windows dropdown menu and then Preferences.

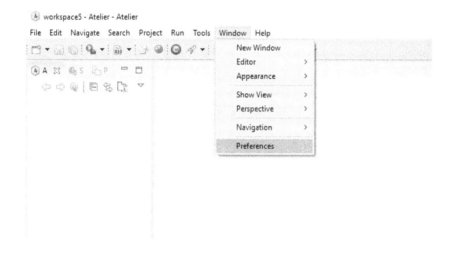

Now select the Automatic Updates.

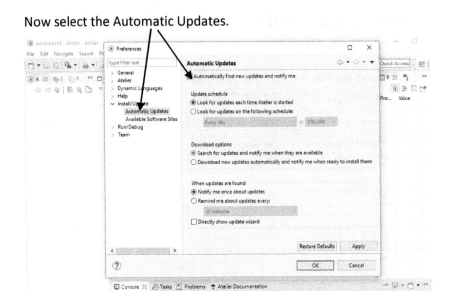

Appendix C – Export and Import

There are two ways to Export or Import Classes or Routines and other types of files.

1) While in the Class or Routine.
2) Using the Export or Import Wizard.

Export while in a Class

While editing a Class, select the File dropdown menu and then Export. The following will be displayed, select XML Caché Script under Atelier Export.

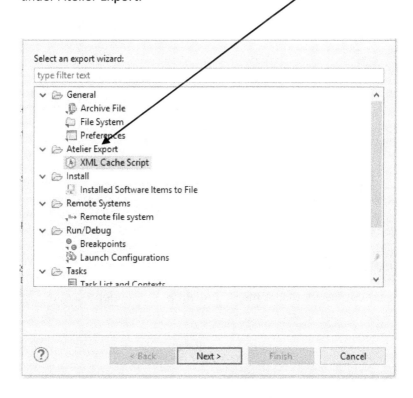

Select an export wizard:

type filter text

- ✓ 🗁 General
  - 🗋 Archive File
  - 🗋 File System
  - 🗋 Preferences
- ✓ 🗁 Atelier Export
  - Ⓐ XML Cache Script
- ✓ 🗁 Install
  - 🗋 Installed Software Items to File
- ✓ 🗁 Remote Systems
  - ↦ Remote file system
- ✓ 🗁 Run/Debug
  - 🔵 Breakpoints
  - 🗋 Launch Configurations
- ✓ 🗁 Tasks
  - 🗋 Task List and Contexts

⑦   < Back   **Next >**   Finish   Cancel

Next you will see the following. This form may be a bit difficult to fill out.

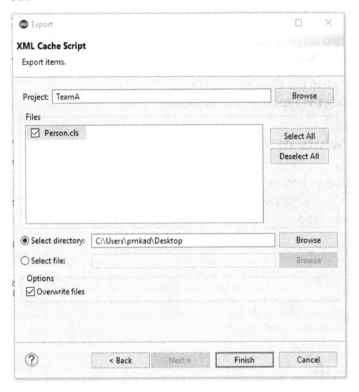

Browse in the Project field until you find the correct Project.

Then select the Class or Select All.

Then put in a directory. Do not put in a file name, that part is a bit confusing. Then hit Finish.

Your output file should be there, it might just be under the name of cls.

Import a Class

Click on the File dropdown menu and select Import. The following will be displayed.

Click on the XML Caché Script.

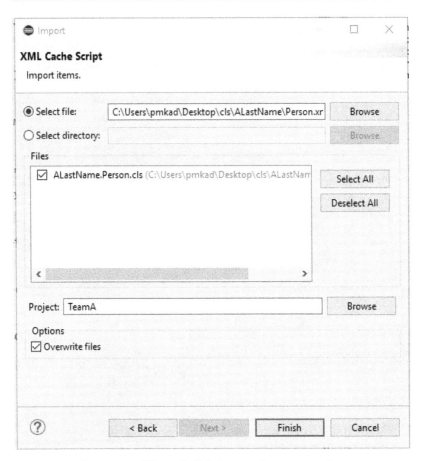

Browse to the correct file and click it, next browse to the correct Project and click on it. Finally click on Finish and the file will be Imported.

Export Classes with the Wizard.

Rarely have I seen the functions for Export and Import as full as what is presented here.

Bring up the Export wizard, from the Workbench → Help dropdown menu → Help Contents → Workbench User Guide → Reference →User Interface Information→Wizards → Export Wizard.

If you left click the Export Wizard you can add this item to your Favorites.

One of the reasons that we added %XML.Adaptor to our classes is to aid in Exports and Imports.

As a developer the items that most interested me are Preferences, XML Caché Script, Run/Debug and Break points.

From here you can use the Export Wizard to choose to Export items from a list:

- ➤ General
  - Archive File
  - File System
  - Preferences
- ➤ Atelier Export
  - XML Caché Script
- ➤ Install
  - Installed Software Items to File
- ➤ Remote Systems
  - Remote file system
- ➤ Run/Debug
  - Breakpoints
  - Launch Configurations
- ➤ Task
  - Task List and Context
- ➤ Team
  - Team Project Set
- ➤ XML
  - XML Catalog

There are pages and pages of documentation on the Import and Export wizards that should help.

A joke is a very serious thing - Winston Churchill.

Appendix D – Atelier Terminal Plugin

With Atelier, there is no native *Terminal* as with Caché. You can obtain a plugin for this function from: *http://download.eclipse.org/tm/terminal/marketplace/.*

However, I suggest that you use the *Terminal* that comes with Studio. Routines and Classes created in Atelier can access the *Terminal* just like Caché Studio.

When the time comes to retire Caché Studio, I expect the *Terminal* function will be left alone, I see no reason to retire it also.

A person without a sense of humor is like a wagon without springs. It's jolted by every pebble on the road –

Henry Ward Beecher.

Appendix E - Regenerate a clean Storage

When you are finished developing your class you should delete the storage and then regenerate it.

If you want the class compiler to generate a clean storage structure, delete the class' storage definition and recompile the class.

You can do this as follows:

- ➤ Open the class in Caché Studio.
- ➤ Right–click on the default Storage definition in the Class Inspector. If the Inspector is not visible, bring it up using Alt+1. Ensure Storage is visible in the left window. Invoke the Delete command in the popup menu.
- ➤ Compile the class. This will cause the class compiler to generate a new storage definition for the class.

Why do you sit there looking like an envelope without any address on it? –

Mark Twain.

Appendix F - Object Commands

Call a class method	
	Do ##class(Package.Class).Method(Params)
	Set Var=##class(Package.Class).Method(Params)
Call a class method	
	Do ##class(Package.Class).Method(Params)
	Set Var=##class(Package.Class).Method(Params)
Create a new object	
	Set Oref=##class(Package.Class).%New(Params)
Save an object	
	Write Oref.%Save()
	Set Status=Oref.%Save()

Validate an Object without Saving	
	Write Oref.%ValidateObject()
	Set Status = Oref.%ValidateObject()
Display an Error	
	Do $SYSTEM.Status.DisplayError(Error)
Remove an Object from memory	
	Set Oref=""
	Kill
Delete an Object from disk	
	Write Set Status=##class(Package.Class).%DeleteId(id)
	Set Status=##class(Package.Class).%DeleteId(id)
Delete all Saved Objects	

	Do ##class(Package.Class).%DeleteExtend() Do ##class(Package.Class).%KillExtent()
Write the value of a Property	
	Write Oref.Property
Write the Id of a saved Object	
	Write Oref.%Id()
Set a Property's value	
	Set Oref.Property=value
Link two Objects	
	Set Oref1.Property=Oref2
Populate a Class	
	Do ##class(Package.Class).Populate(count) This will only work if the properties have POPSPEC parameters

List all Objects in-memory	
	Do $SYSTEM.OBJ.ShowObjects() – pass a "d" for details
List all Properties in an Object	
	Do $SYSTEM.OBJ.Dump(oref)
Start SQL Shell	
	Do $SYSTEM.SQL.Shell()
Run a Class Query	
	Do ##class(%ResultSet).RunQuery(class.query)

Appendix G – Comments

Caché ObjectScript supports several types of comments. Perhaps the easiest is:

Comment Lines

```
Set X=1        ; this is a comment line
Set Y=10       ; from the semicolon to end of line
; semicolon must start at least in column 2

Set X=1        // This is a comment line
Set Y=10       // from the slash-slash to end line
; slash-slash must start at least in column 2
```

Comment Block

```
/*  start of a block of comment
comments
comments
comments
*/ end of a block of comments
```

There are more comments specifications in the InterSystems documentation.

From the Caché Cube → Documentation → Home → Caché Development Guides → Using Caché Studio → Language Elements → Comments.

No comment.

Appendix H – Content Assist

Content assist gives you the functionality to insert a tag, a structure, a property, parameter, resource, function, a line of code, or any number of programming resources.

Most, if not all structured text editors within Eclipse have the *content assist* functionality.

The whole capability for using content assist provides much in the way of programming capabilities and should be learned extensively.

To invoke Content Assist

Position your cursor between the { and }

Go to the Edit dropdown menu and click on Content Assist.

Then either type Ctrl+Space or click on the Default button. It may take a few tries to get it correct. But you should be able to select which parameter you want.

Content Assist gives you a template of what you need. From the *As Type* to the *///documentation* on the line before.

It provides you with a number of templates, for example:

- ➢ #Define – define a preprocessor command
- ➢ #If #Ifelse #else #endif
- ➢ Class
- ➢ ClassMethod
- ➢ Classref
- ➢ Do While
- ➢ For
- ➢ For List
- ➢ For Loop
- ➢ If Construct
- ➢ If Else If Else
- ➢ Try-Catch
- ➢ Property
- ➢ Parameter

Content Assist can be used in a number of different ways.

Appendix I – MUMPS or Caché?

The following is my opinion and my opinion only. If you dislike what I am saying you are free to skip this Appendix.

There are some who feel that MUMPS is an out–of–date system from the 1960s. I know of no group of developers who are still using MUMPS circa 1960. The various MUMPS systems for both database and programming language have been updated and improved over the years. MUMPS has been accused of having a cryptic programming style, which may be true depending upon who writes the code. However, it is only cryptic to non–MUMPS programmers, to MUMPS programmers it is clear as day. The same cryptic charge can be made at Java or C, C+, C++ and other programing language. It is only cryptic to non–programmers.

What is Caché?

So then, what is Caché? Caché is a product of InterSystems Corporation. InterSystems has inveloped a number of MUMPS stove-pipe type of systems as well as larger systems like Digital Standard MUMPS, DSM. InterSystems took these MUMPS systems, updated them, merged them together, added Object Technology, Web Interfaces and a number of others and renamed this conglomerate "Caché." This was not an easy task by any means. They are the largest dog in the fight in the MUMPS/Caché world.

Where is the Problem?

So, where is the problem? There are some who still feel that MUMPS is an archaic system and as such does not warrant consideration. There are others who engage in revisionist history to deny their rich MUMPS background. What a shame, those who wish to deny the background that MUMPS brings to the table ignore the string of successful business victories and problems they have solved over the years, especially in the Healthcare field and the

Veterans Administration, who still call their occupation, MUMPS
Programmers, much to the chagrin of others who hate the word
"MUMPS."

MUMPS will be around for years to come

Whatever you call it, MUMPS or Caché is a major player in business
today, that much cannot be denied. I have been a programmer in
MUMPS and Caché for over 30 years and am proud to be associated
with both names. I dare say that despite the critics that proclaim
that MUMPS and Caché will be around long past those who say it is
old and feeble.

Appendix J – Lexicon

Caché

Spelled properly, Caché should have the acute accent (´) above the "e". Without the accent, the word (Cache) means temporary or memory storage.

Caché is pronounced cash–shay, emphasis on the second syllable.

How do I write the é in the word Caché?

Write the word "Caché" with Cut and Paste

You could find the word Caché on the InterSystems website. Then double–click the word Caché to select it, next, right click the word Caché and copy it into your paste buffer. From there you can paste it whenever you need it.

Write the word Caché in Terminal

You could use Caché's Terminal with:

```
Write "Cach"_$Char(233)
```

```
USER>Write "Cach"_$Char(233)
Caché
USER>
```

Write the word "Caché" in Microsoft Word

Or, if you are using Microsoft Word, in the Ribbon at the top of the page, select Insert. At the far right click on Symbols or More Symbols. You will find the é under Font:(normal text) and Sublet:Latin–1 Supplement.

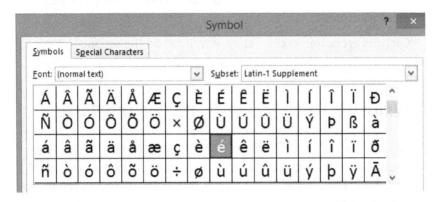

In Microsoft Word, you can get Caché inserted automatically every time you type Cache. In the File Menu, under Options and then Proofing, select the AutoCorrect Options and add an item whereby every time you type Cache it will be replaced with Caché. It will help to have Caché in your copy buffer (so you can just paste it in) before you start. Be sure you have the correct accent. Not the grave accent (à è ì ò ù), but the acute accent (á é í ó ú).

Appendix K - Methods of Translation

What I call Methods of Translation, InterSystems calls Property Methods. These are methods that are created automatically for every Property in a Class. These Methods create automatic translations for the Property. The Methods can be invoked by the developer in appropriate situations.

See the InterSystems Cube → Documentation → Home → Caché Development Guides → Using Caché Objects → Defining Datatype Classes → Overview of Datatype Classes → Property Methods

Some of the Methods of Translation or Property Methods are

- LogicalToDisplay,
- DisplayToLogical,
- LogicalToODBC, and
- ODBCToLogical.

As shown in the documentation, the property or P1 are pre-pended to the Property Methods.

As shown in the documentation:

- P1IsValid(),
- P1Normalize(),
- P1LogicalToDisplay(), and
- P1ToDisplayToLogical(),
- and there are others.

Well?

Glossary

- **$SYSTEM.OBJ.DisplayError(Status)** - method to display an error. Just pass the error code in the Status field.

  For example: Write $SYSTEM.OBJ.DisplayError**(0)**

```
USER>Write $SYSTEM.OBJ.DisplayError(0)

ERROR #00: (no error description)1
USER>Write $SYSTEM.OBJ.DisplayError(3)

WARNING(3) #00: (no error description)1
USER>Write $SYSTEM.OBJ.DisplayError(311011111)

ERROR #5034: Invalid status code structure (311011111)1
USER>
```

- **Atelier** - Atelier is InterSystems' Eclipse-based development environment. It enables you to rapidly build solutions that leverage the performance, scalability, connectivity, and reliability of the InterSystems Data Platform.
- **Atelier Working Sets** - adjustments and changes depending upon what a developer is working on, in other words, predefined preferences for a specific project.
- **BitMap** – a special index that uses a series of bitstrings to be the set of ID values.
- **BitSlice** - a special index that enables very fast evaluation of certain expressions.
- **Caché** - is a commercial Multidimensional object–oriented database management system from InterSystems, used to develop software in many business fields. Applications can use the database with object and SQL code. Caché also allows developers to directly manipulate its underlying data structures: hierarchical arrays known as M technology
- **Caché Objects** – the Caché object model is based upon the ODMG* standard. Caché supports a full array of object programming concepts, including encapsulation, embedded objects, multiple inheritance, polymorphism, and collections –

from *The Caché Technology Guide.* Website:
http://www.intersystems.com/our-products/cache/tech-guide/introduction/

➢ **Caché Technology Guide** – a document explaining InterSystems Caché's approach to Technology. See Website:
http://www.intersystems.com/our–products/cache/tech–guide/introduction/

➢ **CheatSheets** – a computer assisted process that helps a developer perform some tasks. See Help → CheatSheets

➢ **Class** - template for creating interrelated objects, variables and methods.

➢ **Class Parameters** - a class parameter defines a value that is the same for all objects of a given class. This value is set when the class is compiled and cannot be altered.

➢ **Class Members** – Properties, Parameters, Methods, Queries, Indices, SQL Triggers, Foreign Keys, Storage, Projections, and XData.

➢ **Console** – display output from various resources.

➢ **COS** - Caché ObjectScript.

➢ **Contextual Help** – in Atelier as you type part of a command or element and then hit Ctrl-Spacebar various options will be displayed based on what you have already typed.

➢ **CVS** - CVS stands for Concurrent Versions System.

➢ **Developer Community** – a community of InterSystems, Caché, Atelier software enthusiasts that share information, code and other data pertinent to InterSystems software.

➢ **DisplayList** – see Enumerated Properties.

➢ **DTL** - Data Transformation Language

➢ **Eclipse** - Eclipse is an Open source development platform which other modular software can "Plug-in" and run as part of Eclipse. It is an IDE.

➢ **Eclipse Community** – a community of Eclipse enthusiasts that share information, code and other data pertinent to Eclipse.

➢ **Enumerated Properties** – Properties that have multiple meanings, one by one. For example: Properties in a Valuelist, M, F and the corresponding DisplayList is Male, Female.

➢ **Extends** – when one class extends another class.

➤ **Global** - A Global is a persistent sparse multidimensional array. It consists of one or more nodes. Each node contains a name and zero or more subscripts. The data stored may be atomic or complex.

➤ **GUI** - *Graphical User Interface*, pronounced "gooey", is a type of interface that allows users to interact with electronic devices through graphical icons and visual indicators such as secondary notation, as opposed to text–based interfaces, typed command labels or text navigation.

➤ **IDE** - an *Integrated Development Environment* is a software application that provides comprehensive facilities to computer programmers for software development. An IDE normally consists of a source code editor, build automation tools and a debugger. Most modern IDEs have intelligent code completion. From Wikipedia

➤ **.INC** – Include files, not routines per se, .INC files contain macro definitions that can be included by .MAC routines.

➤ **Indices** – three kinds of indices in a class, 1. Standard, 2. BipMap and 3. BitSlice

➤ **Inspector -** Alt+1 will bring up the inspector to view the Class Members in Caché Studio.

➤ **Instance Method** - a Method tied to an Oref (Object Reference). The Method cannot be executed unless through or based upon the Oref.

➤ **.INT** – Intermediate source files, which are compiled directly into executable Caché ObjectScript (OBJ) code. When the Caché macro preprocessor compiles a .MAC routine, it is saved as a .INT file.

➤ **Instance** - an example or single occurrence of something.

➤ **Instantiate** - to create an occurrence of an object class. To cause to "come alive" or be active in-memory.

➤ **Java** - a general purpose computer programming language that is concurrent, class–based, object–oriented, and specifically designed to have as few implementation dependencies as possible. Website: *https://www.java.com/en/download/*

➤ **Keybindings** – in Atelier type Ctrl-Shift-L twice to see all 300+ keybindings from the Workbench.

- **Legacy applications or systems** - an old method, technology, computer system, or application program, previous or outdated computer system. Often a pejorative term, referencing a system as "legacy" means that it paved the way for the standards that would follow it. This can also imply that the system is out of date or in need of replacement.
- **Mapping Globals to Classes** – see chapter 16.
- **Methods** – there are two types of Object Methods: (1) Instance Method - a Method tied to an Oref (Object Reference) and (2) Class Method – a Method not tied to an Oref (Object Reference).
- **Method** - code associated with a class or object to perform a task.
- **MUMPS** - *Massachusetts General Hospital Utility Multi-Programming System*, also known as M, is a general-purpose computer programming language that gives ACID (Atomic, Consistent, Isolated, and Durable) transaction processing. Its most unique and differentiating feature is its "built-in" database, enabling high-level access to disk storage using simple symbolic program variables and subscripted arrays, like the variables used by most computer programming languages.
- **Namespace** - a logical representation of data, while a database is a physical representation. A Namespace can cover multiple databases, or it can cover a part of a database. It can also be local and or remote.
- **ODBC** - *Open Database Connectivity* that can access any kind of database management system (DBMS).
- **ODBC** - a low level, high performance interface that is designed specifically for relational data stores.
- **ODMG** - *Object Data Management Group* – developed the original standard for object databases.
  See Website: *http://www.odbms.org/odmg-standard/*
- **Objects** - a language mechanism for binding data with methods that operate on that data.
- **Object Code** - a sequence of statements or instructions in a computer language, usually a machine code language.

➢ **Object Technology** - An umbrella term for object oriented programming, object oriented databases, and object oriented design methodologies.

➢ **Object–Oriented Programming** - (OOP) is a programming language model organized around objects rather than "actions" and data rather than logic. Traditionally a program has been viewed as a logical procedure that takes input data, processes it, and produces output data.

➢ **OLE** - OLE allows an editing application to export part of a document to another editing application and then import it with additional content. For example, a desktop publishing system might send some text to a word processor or a picture to a bitmap editor using OLE. The main benefit of OLE is to add different kinds of data to a document from different applications, like a text editor and an image editor. This creates a Compound File Binary Format document and a master file to which the document makes reference. Changes to data in the master file immediately affect the document that references it. This is called "linking" (instead of "embedding").

➢ **Query** – there are two types of Queries, 1. Basic Class Query and 2. Custom Class Query. The Basic Class Query is show in Chapter 16.

➢ **Outline View** – a View that assist in viewing a Class Properties.

➢ **Output** - Alt+2 will bring up the output from the code Caché Studio.

➢ **OOP** – Object Oriented Programming.

➢ **ObjectScript** - one of Caché's Programming Languages.

➢ **Oref** - *Object Reference*, or a pointer to an Object Reference. When an object is created, Caché creates an in–memory structure of the object.

➢ **Outline** – is a different way of looking at resources and other items in Eclipse.

➢ **Parameters** – or Class Parameter – A class parameter defines a value that is the same for all objects of a given class. This value is established when the class is compiled and cannot be altered. Or in other words holds constant data.

➢ **Properties** - class member that defines the state of an object. Or class members that holds data.

- ➤ **Property Keywords** – keywords are: Required, InitialExpression, Transient, Private, Calculated, MultiDimensional
- ➤ **Preference** - settings in Atelier that specifies your choices.
- ➤ **Project** - a project is an individual or collaborative enterprise, involving research, design, and programming, that is carefully planned, usually by a project team, to achieve a particular aim. A **project** may also be a set of interrelated tasks to be executed over a fixed period and within certain cost and other limitations.
- ➤ **Queries** – two kinds of queries in a class 1. Basic Class Query, 2. Custom Class Query.
- ➤ **Quick Access Box** – a box in the upper right-hand corner of the Workbench. As you click inside the box it says, "Start typing to search commands and more . . . "
- ➤ **Resources** – collectively: Perspectives, Views, Editors, Windows, Files, and Folders.
- ➤ **SQL** - the acronym for *Structured Query Language*, is a standardized computer language that was originally developed by IBM for querying, altering, and defining relational databases, using declarative statements.
- ➤ **SQL Trigger** - A SQL Trigger specifies that upon an Event (Insert, Update or Delete) that some defined action should be taken. An example of a SQL Trigger is shown in chapter 16.
- ➤ **Storage** - Alt+4 will bring up the Storage display in Caché Studio.
- ➤ **Studio** - an IDE for developing Routines, Classes, etc. that would access the Caché database.
- ➤ **Support Center** - InterSystems' Worldwide Support Center, Telephone: +1–617–621–0700, Fax: +1–616–374–9391, Email: *support@InterSystems.com*.
- ➤ **Workbench** – the Eclipse/Atelier desktop environment.
- ➤ **Workspace** - Alt+1 will bring up the Workspace to in Caché Studio.
- ➤ **Workspace Directory** – the directory on disk that holds all the Eclipse/Atelier information necessary for any one project.
- ➤ **ValueList** – see Enumerated Properties.
- ➤ **View** – a view is a structure that supports editors and other resources and provides primary and alternative presentations as

well as ways to navigate the information in your Workbench within Eclipse

➤ **XML** - *eXtensible Markup Language*, XML was designed to describe a document structure or the data structure so that it is both machine and human readable.

When you go to the mind reader, do you get half price? –

David Letterman.

Index

I am free of all prejudices. I hate everyone equally –

W. C. Fields.

Books by Paul Mike Kadow

Caché ObjectScript & MUMPS - 2012

Paperback on Amazon.com, 8.5" X 11" 512 pages

This book serves as an explanation of Caché ObjectScript and the MUMPS programming language. It is designed as both a comprehensive learning guide and a technical reference manual. This is useful to programmers of any level, whether you are new to the language or an experienced developer looking for more information on Caché Objects, containing hundreds of code examples . . . the perfect desk top reference.

From the Forward of *Caché ObjectScript and MUMPS*

This book is written for all those who want a Caché ObjectScript/Caché Objects and MUMPS book for the beginner. Although it starts from the very basic commands, it does progress to the point that even the most experienced programmer will learn. It is not an exhaustive treatment of the subjects covered. It serves as a desktop reference with many examples, the concepts are taught (as far as possible) through examples.

Caché ObjectScript and MUMPS has over 700 examples and goes into much detail. The examples are still available for download at *http://www.cosmumps.org*. Or contact me at *mike@cosmumps.org*.

Paperback and Kindle on Amazon.com, 6" x 9" 528 pages

This book chronicles and explores some of the many areas InterSystems has grown into and has influenced over the years.

In addition, there are multiple chapters on Globals, Classes, SQL/Query, etc. This book explores Routine Elements, Routine Structures, Caché Studio, Studio Debugger, and Routine Extras as well as a section on *Cheat Sheets* and calling System Methods & Queries. It also embodies several chapters on Caché Developer Resources that list other groups, companies, software, websites, learning centers, courses, programs, documentation and the like that gives the Caché developer a leg up. It embodies a number of other companies and software reviews that will give the developer a sense of history and what is currently available.

In simple and straightforward fashion, this book documents the concepts, commands, and functions of Caché ObjectScript, Caché Routines, Caché Studio, Globals, Objects, Classes, and SQL.

Biography

Mike Kadow

My career in computing started after I graduated from San Jose State University with a degree in Accounting. The trouble was no one was interested in hiring me as an Accountant. I did get this call from EDS (Electronic Data Systems). They called me because I was a Veteran. Well, 3 years playing Alto Sax in the U.S. Army Band did not seem like a real Veteran to me, but it did count.

EDS wanted to hire me, train me in computing (it was called "Data Processing" back then) and put me in a job writing computer programs, sure sounded good to me so I said yes.

My career as a programmer started with a 3-year stent at EDS, first I spent some time on the client's side learning what it was like being a client, then six months attending EDS's famous computer school and finally two years plus in San Francisco.

I wanted to move to the east coast, so I started looking. DEC (Digital Equipment Corporation) picked me up for the next 20 years. It was there in 1985 I was introduced to MUMPS, well my mentor was really trained in MIIS. At DEC, MUMPS was called DSM (Digital Standard MUMPS). At DEC, we had a large DSM group supporting the CIC (Country Information Center) which supported a number of Digital's Management Systems.

I did not see it coming but the CIC application at DEC started winding down. On my 20th anniversary at DEC, I received my layoff notice. After 23 years plus of straight employment I entered the contracting field. At the same time, I started my first book, *Caché ObjectScript and MUMPS*. My down time from contracting provided me with plenty of time to work on my book and to maintain my sanity.

I did find contracting rather painful, yes, the pay was good, what was not good was being away from home and family.

Finally, I landed a long-term contract where I could work from home and it was during that time that I managed to complete my first book after 12 years of effort. I was working for CACI at the time.

Biography

In 2012 I published *Caché ObjectScript and MUMPS.*

Shortly thereafter, I landed in the hospital for five months with multiple back surgeries.

In 2016 I published *Caché and MUMPS – Part II.* At the same time working for CACI and ByLight off and on.

In 2018 I published *Caché Object with Atelier.*

Soli Deo Gloria

My Testimony

Some may say that my testimony has no place in a technical book as this, however, whether it belongs here or not, I am compelled to give it.

I joined the US Army in July of 1968. During Basic Training I was reading from *Good News for Modern Man*, a New Testament someone had given to me. I was reading from the passages about many are called but few are chosen.

Then one Sunday afternoon word came down regarding some event on the Parade Grounds, we were told it was not mandatory but "you will be there." We were all there and someone was talking to us about Jesus Christ. An invitation was given, and I found myself going forward.

A week or so later I had a meeting with a Chaplain Johnson, He kept stressing this verse in the Bible, Revelation 3:20, "Behold, I stand at the door and knock. If anyone hears my voice and opens the door, I will come in to him and eat with him, and he with me". I was not sure what the Chaplain was talking about, nor what Jesus was talking about in the verse. But whatever it was, I wanted it. Several nights later, I invited Jesus into my life.

A few weeks later, I arrived at my next duty station, it was the Naval School of Music in Norfolk Virginia, and I was preparing for the US Army Band. I knew I was a Christian, not sure how I knew but I did. I also knew that Christians attend Bible Studies. So, I found a Bible Study listed on the bulletin board. I went to the Study and it was there I met Fred (not his real name), Fred was a chief in the Navy. Fred took an interest in me and invited me to his home for the weekend. I had no other offers, being 3000 miles away from home, so I accepted. I remember on the drive to his house he kept asking me questions about my choosing Christ.

The next morning Fred had somewhere to go so he sat me down and had me listen to a tape on Scripture Memory. And with that, I started my Christian life.

If you have never considered what a Christian is, there is no time like the present. You could die tonight in your sleep and find yourself standing before the God of all creation. If you feel Christ tugging at your heart, repent and turn to God and never look back.

Revelation 3:20 "Behold, I stand at the door and knock. If anyone hears my voice and opens the door, I will come in to him and eat with him, and he with me. " Amen and Amen.

The End